Bringing God Home

Family Devotions
for the Christian Year

Bringing God Home

Family Devotions
for the Christian Year

James L. Evans

SMYTH & HELWYS
PUBLISHING, INC.

Macon, Georgia

ISBN 1-57312-014-6

Bringing God Home
Family Devotions for the Christian Year
James L. Evans

Copyright ©1995
Smyth & Helwys Publishing, Inc.®
6316 Peake Road
Macon, Georgia 31210-3960
1-800-568-1248

All biblical quotations are taken from the
New Revised Standard Version (NRSV) unless
otherwise indicated.

Library of Congress Cataloging-in-Publication Data

Evans, James L., 1952–
    Bringing God home: family devotions for the Christian year (Year A)/ James L. Evans.
    xii + 228   8" x 8"
    Contents:
    ISBN 1-57312-014-6
    1. Family–Prayer: books and devotions–English. 2. Church year–Prayer: books and
    devotions–English. I. Title.
        BV255.E93 1995   95-23772
        249–dc20   CIP

Contents

Bringing God Home

Preface

Home worship is not a new idea. Centuries before either the temple or the synagogue appeared in Hebrew history, faithful families worshipped God in their homes. The people of Israel understood the importance of home prayer and instruction. In fact, Hebrew parents assumed the primary role for teaching and leading their children in worship.

> Hear, O Israel: The Lord is our God, the Lord alone. You shall love the Lord your God with all your heart, with all your soul, and with all your might. Keep these words that I am commanding you today in your heart. Recite them to your children and talk about them when you are at home and when you are away, when you lie down and when you rise. Bind them as a sign on your hand, fix them as an emblem on your forehead, and write them on the doorposts of your house and on your gates. (Deut 6:4-9)

The successful results of this early family worship is preserved for all time in the stories and poetry that make up the canon of the Hebrew Bible. These family efforts made it possible for an important religious heritage to pass from parent to child along with all the other family treasures. Even when more institutional forms of worship began to dominate Hebrew spiritual life, the emphasis on prayer and instruction in the home remained. This fact accounts for the close connection between home worship and the early progress of Christianity.

As the early church struggled for existence and identity, in the homes of faithful men and women the gospel story was told and re-told. The apostle Paul contends that he preached his message from house to house (Acts 20:20). This emphasis on home worship became a pattern even away from Jewish influence. Churches throughout the Greek world were firmly established in homes (Acts 2:2; 46; Rom 16:5; 1 Cor 16:9).

In our day, worship is more formal and mainly institutional in nature. When people think of a service of worship, they probably envision a building specifically set aside and equipped for that purpose. Our time is also marked by a reliance upon professionals. We depend on people specially trained to perform worship functions on our behalf. The net result is a sad reduction in the practice of home worship.

The consequences of this reduction are serious. The home has a crucial role to play in the lives of local congregations. Clark Hemsley, a family enrichment leader for Baptists in Mississippi, says The temperature in local churches is controlled by thermostats in the home. This is not to say that we should abandon our church buildings and worship in our own backyards. That sort of isolation has its own problems. On the contrary, an emphasis on home worship strengthens the work of the local church. Both settings for worship are essential. One undergirds the other.

First, home worship helps everyone, and especially children, to learn how to worship. Certain aspects of worship may be innate. All people seem to have a longing for the divine presence, but the practice of worship is a discipline that must be learned and therefore taught. The most natural setting for this to occur is in the home. Furthermore, by means of regular home worship, children and adults learn the importance of active involvement in worship. Modern experiences of worship tend toward the character of spectator events. This cannot be. Worship calls for the best of our hearts, minds, and souls. Worship is a participatory activity. We cannot simply watch it happen; we must be actively involved.

Home worship also serves to illustrate the centrality of worship in our lives as God's people. One of the greatest mistakes we make as Christians is separating our spiritual lives from the rest of our lives. If our Christianity only has application on Sunday, then it simply becomes one more obligation tacked onto our busy lives. If our faith is something central in our lives, however, something that makes our lives complete, then worship takes on a profound dimension. When our children see us worship not only on Sunday, but also daily, they will gain the distinct impression that loving and serving God is something we take seriously.

For families with children, the teaching function of home worship becomes critical. When we take time to read the Bible and teach its truth using creative and authentic methods, the home becomes the perfect setting for passing along our religious heritage. Children will do what they see us doing. Why not let them see us worshiping and living out the meaning of our faith? Jesus made it clear that life is best lived when focused around a central truth: **Love God with all your hearts and love your neighbor as yourself** (Mark 12:30). The first step toward making this central truth a priority in our own lives begins in the act of worship in the home.

What is the best way to accomplish home worship? Who in the modern world has time to come up with daily or weekly worship activities that will be interesting and helpful? How can we address the developmental needs of children and teenagers while at the same time maintaining integrity with the message of the Scriptures? These questions are vital, but not insurmountable.

Churches in the liturgical tradition already possess many resources for meeting the challenges of home worship. The lectionary, a collection of readings or selections from the Scriptures arranged for proclamation and worship, is the center piece of these resources. Lectionaries have been in use for centuries. They provide an orderly and systematic presentation of the salient elements of our faith story and connect the Old and New Testaments. Lectionaries are not intended to limit or control what the church may hear. On the contrary, churches that follow the cycle of readings will ultimately hear more of the canon of Scripture than those churches that rely on the personal preference of local leaders.

Since the mid-1960s, many churches have shared a commitment to the Common Lectionary. Among them are: churches the Anglican tradition, the Disciples of Christ, the Episcopal church, the Lutheran Church in America, the Evangelical Lutheran Church in America and Canada, the Free Methodist Church in Canada, The Lutheran Church–Missouri Synod, Polish National Catholic Church, Presbyterian Church (U.S.A.), the Presbyterian Church in Canada, Reformed Church in America, Roman Catholic Church in the United States and Canada, The United Church of Canada, United Church of Christ, the United Methodist Church, and many Baptist congregations.

The Common Lectionary follows the pattern of ancient lectionaries. The cycle of readings is based on the life of Jesus and follows the seasons and celebrations of the Christian year. Because of this, the Gospel reading almost always establishes the theme for the selection of texts. The Scripture readings are divided into three-year cycles. These years are designated as Year A, Year B, and Year C. Year A features the Gospel of Matthew. Year B features the Gospel of Mark. Year C features the Gospel of Luke. The Gospel of John is interspersed into the cycle of readings throughout the three-year cycle. As churches or families follow the lectionary readings, they discover they are following Jesus as he made his way toward the cross. His life, death, and resurrection, along with the heart of his teaching, provide a map for us to follow through time with our own lives.

In the introduction to the Revised Common Lectionary (1992), the Consultation on Common Texts explains some of the intended uses of a common lectionary. In addition to providing churches and denominations with a uniform and common pattern of biblical proclamation, the Common Lectionary also serves as a guide for church leaders, the development of Bible study curriculum, and finally,

> as a guide to individuals and groups who wish to read, study, and pray the Bible in tune with the church's prayer and preaching. Some local churches print the references to the following Sunday's reading in their bulletins and encourage people to come prepared for the next week's celebration.[1]

Bringing God Home: Family Devotions for the Christian Year is an effort to fulfill this final objective. Using the Common Lectionary as a scriptural guide, this book will serve as a resource for conducting home worship for Year A. Cultivating a discipline of home worship will lead to a renewed appreciation for the Bible as well as for worship itself. Families with children will find this book especially helpful. Children learn best when they are actively involved with the subject matter. Little boys and girls do not sit still very long for anyone—even Mom and Dad. Therefore, the best way to help children worship and learn the Bible at home is to conduct the worship in such a way that they are able to touch it, smell it, taste it, hold it, and hear it.

Our ultimate goal is to enrich and facilitate home worship. One of the goals of all Christian parents is to help their children develop an authentic faith. We know that authentic faith cannot be forced or coerced; it is a choice. As parents, however, we are in a unique teaching position. We have opportunities to guide our children so that they at least understand their choices. Families who worship together and practice a discipline of study and reflection are not guaranteed success or immunity from the ills that plague our world. They are, however, provided with an opportunity to consider a life much deeper and satisfying than empty alternatives promoted by advertisers. Along the way, they will enjoy the rich and enjoyable pleasure of celebrating God's presence in their home. If there is hope for our world and for our children, this may be where it begins.

How to Use the Book

The readings and activities outlined in this book follow the cycle of the Christian year. Therefore, we begin with Advent in Year A. Since the purpose of these worship activities is to prepare us for the service of worship in our churches, the reading and activities will always be one week ahead. In other words, we will always be moving towards the coming Sunday. The Psalm, the Old Testament reading, the Epistle, and the Gospel that we study at the beginning of the week will likely be the readings in the service of worship on Sunday.

As we study the Scriptures and work through the learning activities, certain ideas or truths will become real for us. We may have questions answered or questions raised. Then, when Sunday comes, the same Scriptures will be dealt with again. Invariably, the emphasis will be a little different. A fresh perspective will be experienced. Other insights will be grasped, perhaps others reinforced. Children will find the service of worship enhanced as parents point out to them that the lessons in the service are the same ones the family has studied the week before. We will experience a sense of connectedness as our private devotions become the subject of hymns, proclamation, and praise.[2]

Using this book as a worship guide is very easy. Each week's outline is basically the same. First, a theme will be assigned to the week. For example, the theme for the First Week of Advent is Waiting. The readings for the week will be listed at the top of the page. After a brief explanation of the assigned theme, a suggested worship plan will be described. This worship plan should be adapted in any way that works with your family's schedule. The basic plan calls for a daily reading and brief activity. If a daily meeting does not work for you, use an alternative plan, or complete the whole week in one day if you wish.

Each of the four scripture readings will have a brief learning exercise. In most instances, an object or activity will be suggested that will serve to illustrate the lesson. The purpose of these exercises will be to involve as many of the senses as possible, insuring that not only are the worship activities interesting, but also memorable. Because families are busier than ever before, time and its use are special concerns for everyone. For that reason, the daily activities are indeed brief. With careful preparation, the daily reading and worship activity can be accomplished in about fifteen minutes.

Friday of each week is suggested as an action day. We will be encouraged as families to find ways to make the lessons of the week real, thereby adding to our worship and spiritual food by putting our faith into practice. The suggested activities might be as simple as baking cookies for a neighbor or as involved as making a visit to someone in a nursing home. These ideas are intended to stimulate your own creativity. The main point, however, is to remember that worship is an act of service, and that loving God also means loving our neighbors.

As we discipline ourselves to study the Bible in a systematic way, we will find our faith growing stronger and experience a sense of renewal in our lives. Our appreciation of congregational worship will grow, and our knowledge of the Scriptures will increase. Perhaps most importantly, for families with children, we will have found a way to pass along a spiritual heritage. More important than any material inheritance is the spiritual legacy we leave behind.

Let us join ourselves to this task as we follow Christ through the year. Let us remember and relive the events of our redemption. Let us mark the gift of days and weeks with meaningful worship and family warmth. If we do these things, we will understand profoundly the words of our Lord, "And remember, I am with you always, to the end of the age" (Matthew 28:20).

Notes

1 *The Revised Common Lectionary,* The Consultation on Common Texts, Includes Complete List of Lections For Years A, B, and C, Abingdon Press: Nashville, 1992, pp. 9-10. (Italics mine.)

2 Even if your church does not follow the lectionary, or regularly use the cycle of readings, families who practice a regular discipline of worship and study at home are going to benefit greatly.

The Meaning of Advent

Besides this, you know what time it is, how it is now the moment for you to wake from sleep. For salvation is nearer to us now than when we became believers. (Romans 13:11)

Advent means "coming." The focus of an Advent celebration is on the birth of Jesus the first coming. The lectionary helps us prepare for this celebration by guiding us through selected Scripture readings. These readings will assist us as we prepare for the gift of God's Son in our own lives.

First Week of Advent[1]
Theme: Waiting

Scripture Readings for the Week
Psalm 122; Isaiah 2:1-5; Romans 13:11-14; and Matthew 24:36-44

Materials Needed
Secure a clock. Begin by explaining what you hope to accomplish with a daily discipline of worship. You may take a few moments and talk about the lectionary. Encourage family members to listen in church Sunday for the Scriptures you have read this week. If you are using the Scriptures as a daily worship guide, the following outline will be helpful.

Monday

Let us go to the house of the LORD! (Psalm 122:1)

Scripture Reading
Psalm 122. Show everyone the clock. After the reading, you might ask, "What time do we have worship?" Allow family members time to respond. Continue by saying, "We know what time church starts, but what time does worship start? Is there a difference? Yes, there is. Worship does not begin when church begins.

Worship begins when we begin to worship God."

That was why the Psalmist was so happy. The writer was active in worshiping God all the time, but when it was time to go into the house of the Lord, that just made it better. Worship did not begin in the house of the Lord, it continued there.

Worship, however, does require one important ingredient: God! We cannot start without God being present. The ancient Hebrews were taught to wait on the Lord, which means being attentive, paying attention. That is true whether we worship in God's house or our house.

Closing Prayer
Close your worship time in prayer. Allow everyone an opportunity to pray. You may pray for people or for special needs. Be sure to express thanksgiving for God's presence in our lives.

_____

_____

_____

_____

_____

_____

Tuesday

Neither shall they learn war any more. (Isaiah 2:4)

Scripture Reading

Isaiah 2:1-5. Use the clock again. Ask family members, "What time is it? Is it present time, past time, or future time?" Allow family members time to respond. Read Isaiah 2:1-5. After the reading, you might say, "The prophet was speaking to his present time about a future time. His people were excited to hear that some time in the future, God would help God's people turn their weapons into tools for growing food. Isaiah was looking forward to a time when the worship of God would bring people together. They would no longer fight, but would turn their tools of war into tools to meet human need."

"Has that happened yet? (Unfortunately, no.) Well then, we will continue to join with other people in waiting and worship until it does happen. Is there anything we can do while we wait?" Allow everyone a chance to voice their own opinion. After a few moments, you might say, "One thing we can do is be sure that we do not contribute to the violence in our world. As we worship and wait, let us seek to contribute to peace."

Closing Prayer

Close your worship time in prayer. Invite family members to pray for peace using their own words.

Family Journal

_____

_____

_____

_____

Wednesday

*You know what time it is, how it is now
the moment for you to wake from sleep. (Romans 13:11)*

Scripture Reading

Romans 13:11-14. After the reading, show everyone the clock. You might say something like, "Why in the world do we need an alarm clock? What is its use?" Allow everyone to have fun discussing the uses of an alarm clock.

Obviously, the purpose of an alarm clock is to wake us from sleep.

"Paul wrote to his friends in Rome to tell them that it was time to wake up. How were they sleeping? The people thought the hope of salvation was something yet to come. They were still waiting for a savior, but Paul knew that God had already sent Jesus into the world to begin the process of redemption.

"Do people today know what God has done for us? Do they know that Jesus is in the world to make things right? How can we be like an alarm clock for those who are sleeping through the message of hope in God's Son?" (Allow for creative responses.)

Closing Prayer

Join hands and invite family members to pray that people who are sleeping through their hope might wake up and find life.

Family Journal

_____

_____

_____

_____

_____

_____

Thursday

But about that day and hour no one knows.
(Matthew 24:36)

Scripture Reading

Matthew 24:36-44. After the reading, you might ask, "What was Jesus talking about?" Allow a few moments for family members to answer. Continue by saying, "Jesus was careful to instruct his disciples in the certainty of the second coming. Jesus made it clear, however, that the date and time of this event was not known to anyone. People who live with the expectation of the fulfillment of all things must do so patiently. Anyone who claims to know the appointed time of the second coming is mistaken. Anyone who gets impatient while waiting misses the point. No one knows the day, but everyone is told how to wait. We are to stay awake!"

Ask family members, "What do you think Jesus meant when he told his disciples to stay awake?" Allow a few moments for them to respond. Continue by making reference to the alarm clock. "Remember yesterday we talked about Paul trying to wake the people of Rome. Well, Jesus was trying to keep his followers awake. Living the life of a Christian means paying attention, doing what is right, and waiting patiently for the fulfillment of God's promises.

"Think of some ways that we might wait and *be awake* at the same time. What do you think God wants us to be doing?" Affirm all responses. Say, "We are waiting for the Lord to appear and for fulfillment, but we are not idle. We have important things to do. We must stay awake and do them."

Closing Prayer
Lead your family in a prayer. Ask for God's guidance as we seek to live our lives in a meaningful way.

Family Journal

_____

_____

_____

_____

_____

_____

Putting Faith into Action!

Briefly review the theme for the week. Suggest that your family join together in an activity that is both helpful and meaningful. Plan to make a family visit to an elderly person in your neighborhood. This person may be a member of your church or a member of your family. Explain to children that often times elderly people experience loneliness and frustration. They are not able to live active lives as they once did. Sometimes they become impatient with their lives and wonder why they are still living. They forget they are supposed to stay awake! A warm visit from caring friends may lighten the load of their day. Call first and make sure it is a convenient time.

Second Week of Advent[2]
Theme: Preparation

Important events in life require special preparation. If something is too easy to do, it may not have lasting value. Really important occasions call for our time and attention. Therefore, as we prepare for Advent for the coming of Jesus into the world there are some things we need to do.

Scripture Readings for the Week
Psalm 72:1-7, 18-19; Isaiah 11:1-10; Romans 15:4-13; and Matthew 3:1-12

Materials Needed
Use a map or globe in your worship times this week.

Monday

May he judge your people with righteousness, and your poor with justice. (Psalm 72:2)

Scripture Reading
Psalm 72:1-7, 18-19. After the reading, call everyone's attention to the map or globe. Be sure it is upside down. The upside down map illustrates the world upside down. What this really means is that things are not as they should be. The Psalmist insisted that the world was upside down when the needs of poor people are not met.

We prepare for the coming of Jesus by working to turn the world right side up. The way we do that is by seeking ways to help the weak and helpless people of our world.

Closing Prayer
Close your worship time in prayer. Ask God to help us turn our world right side up and to show us ways to help those in need.

Family Journal

_____

_____

_____

_____

_____

Tuesday

The wolf shall live with the lamb . . .
and a little child shall lead them.(Isaiah 11:6)

Scripture Reading

Isaiah 11:1-10. Show everyone the map or globe again. Say something like, "Few places in this world are free of war or violence. God did not make the world for us to fight over it, but for us to live in it." Ask family members to name things they would be willing to fight for. Allow time for discussion.

Continue by saying, "The prophet saw a future time when people would live on earth without fear. There would be no danger from either human threat or from wild animals. We still wait for this future peace, but we prepare for it by working for peace now." Ask family members, "How can we work for peace? One simple way is to refuse to fight among ourselves."

Closing Prayer

Close your worship time in prayer. Ask God to help us wait for the future without hurting each other.

Family Journal

_____

_____

_____

_____

_____

Wednesday

Welcome one another, therefore, just as Christ
has welcomed you, for the glory of God. (Romans 15:7)

Scripture Reading

Romans 15:4-13. Point out on the globe or map all the different lines. Some lines are latitude and longitude. These lines divide the world into location zones. Other lines represent borders. These lines divide the world into states and countries. Some divisions are good, but some divisions are bad they hurt us.

Encourage family members to think of divisions that may be bad for us. If children are young, you may need to help them. For instance, dividing children at school into friends and not friends. Other examples may include race, gender, or social divisions.

What can we do to remove some of the bad barriers that exist in our world? What does our text for today suggest? Refer to the map or globe again. Say something like, "The lines in the world often separate us and make us enemies with other people. Jesus died so that the world might become a community of hope."

Closing Prayer

Close your worship time with prayer. Let family members pray in their own words. Ask God to help us remove all unnecessary dividing lines.

Family Journal

_____
_____
_____
_____
_____
_____
_____

Thursday

Prepare the way of the Lord,
make his paths straight. (Matt 3:3; Isaiah 40:3)

Scripture Reading

Matthew 3:1-12. After the reading, refer to the map or globe. Explain how the map distinguishes between mountains and plains. Say something like, "Our world is not a flat and even place. There are bumpy spots in our world. The same is true for life. John the Baptist said that one way we prepare for Jesus' coming was by dealing with the bumpy places. We deal with them by repentance, which means to turn around, to find a different way."

Use the map to illustrate what you are saying. Chart a course from one place to another. Talk about how you will avoid difficult travel areas. These turns and detours are the repentance of travel. In life we also make many starts, turns, and start overs.

Continue by saying, "As we wait for Jesus to arrive, we must prepare ourselves. We must be on the right road, although the road may be bumpy and rough. Occasionally, it is rough because of poor decisions we have made. In any case, the solution is the same. Repent and find a better way the way of the Lord."

Closing Prayer

Close your worship time in silence. Then, ask God to help us make good decisions and go in the right direction while we wait for the bumpy places to become smooth.

Family Journal

_____

_____

_____

_____

_____

Putting Faith into Action!

Bake a cake for a friend. Be sure to note the careful steps and careful preparation needed for the cake to turn out properly. Preparation is even necessary in order to deliver the cake. The friend must be called and a time arranged. Point out that if something as simple as baking a cake for a friend requires this much preparation, how much more should we take seriously the call to prepare for the coming of Jesus.

Third Week of Advent[3]
Theme: Gratitude

Scripture Readings for the Week

Psalm 146:5-10; Isaiah 35:1-10; James 5:7-10; Matthew 11:2-11

Materials Needed

Thank you notes will be used as teaching tools this week.

Monday

Praise the LORD! (Psalm 146:10)

Scripture Reading

Psalm 146:5-10. After the reading, show everyone the thank you notes you have provided. (If you do not have thank you notes on hand, explain to family members how thank you notes work. Use paper and pencils to make your own.)

If we are willing to send thank you notes to people who are kind or helpful to us, how can we overlook God? Of course, we cannot send a note to God, but we can express thanks like the Psalmist. By voicing our praise and gratitude, we are showing an appropriate thankful attitude for all that God has done for us.

Closing Prayer

As we wait for Jesus to come at Christmas, being thankful is an important part of our wait. Close your worship by expressing gratitude to God for God's goodness.

Family Journal

_____

_____

_____

_____

_____

_____

Tuesday

They shall see the glory of the LORD, the majesty of our God. (Isaiah 35:2)

Scripture Reading

Isaiah 35:1-10. After the reading, say something like, "When we write a thank you note to someone, we are usually very specific about what we are thanking them for. It is important that we be specific when we thank God, too. If we are not careful, we will say something like, 'Thank you God for everything.' Genuine thanks knows what we are being thankful for.

"The prophet Isaiah knew this. He knew that as the people of Israel waited for the Messiah, they would grow dry and thirsty in their wait just like a desert. When the Messiah came, however, he would bring refreshing water, set captive people free, end pain and suffering, and give a reason for thankfulness."

Closing Prayer
Let's be faithful to write thank you notes to God, but let's also be specific and name what it is we are thankful for. (Take a few moments and do this now.) Write down your prayer of thanks!

Family Journal

_____
_____
_____
_____
_____
_____

Wednesday

Be patient, therefore, beloved,
until the coming of the Lord. (James 5:7)

Scripture Reading
James 5:7-10. After the reading, you might say something like, "We have talked about several ways of saying thanks. Our text today offers us an opportunity to show thanks. We show our gratitude to God when we patiently endure hard situations."

Invite family members to express what they think patience means. Also allow family members, especially children, to think of instances where they experienced pain, frustration, or disappointment. These are times that call for patience. Continue by saying, "But why does this show gratitude? If we live life grumbling and complaining about what we don't have, it is obvious we do not value what we do have. Failing to be patient says to God, 'What you have provided is not good enough.' That is not a thankful attitude."

Closing Prayer
Close your worship time in prayer. Express thanks to God for the life God has given us as it is.

Family Journal

_____

_____

_____

_____

_____

Thursday

Yes, I tell you, and more than a prophet. (Matthew 11:9)

Scripture Reading

Matthew 11:2-11. After the reading, you might say, "John the Baptist was in prison. It was easy for people to look at him and say, 'Well his life did not turn out too well.'

"Jesus, however, would not allow such attitudes to exist. Even though John was in prison, Jesus reminded his friends that John was a faithful servant. One of the ways we show gratitude to God is by showing gratitude for God's servants."

Encourage family members to think about the different people who serve you and your family. Include persons at grocery stores, gas stations, and restaurants. Don't forget doctors, nurses, and ministers. Someone in your family may serve in the military. This, too, is an important form of service.

Closing Prayer

Take a few moments and give thanks to God for the people who serve you. Allow everyone an opportunity to pray.

Family Journal

_____

_____

_____

_____

_____

Putting Faith into Action!

Remind everyone of the thank you notes we started the week with. You might say something like, "We can't really write God a thank you note. We can say thank you in prayer, but we cannot write God." Continue by saying, "We can, however, be sure that we take note of the service of others." Write a thank you note to someone who has served you or your family in a special way. You may want to send different notes from different members of the family, or one note from the whole family. Be sure to say, "We thank God for the way you serve us."

Fourth Week of Advent
Theme: God With Us

Scripture Readings for the Week
Psalm 80:1-7, 17-19; Isaiah 7:10-16; Romans 1:1-7;
Matthew 1:18-25

Materials Needed
Provide markers and paper for everyone. Invite family members to make signs or small posters that illustrate how God is near to us. Be prepared to offer suggestions or have your own poster already made so children will have an idea of what you are asking them to do. If your children cannot write, allow them to draw God with us. Feature a different poster each day of your worship. Prepare a poster that says, "Jesus is God's Son!" This poster will be used on Wednesday.

Monday

Restore us, O God of hosts; let your face shine,
that we may be saved. (Psalm 80:7)

Scripture Readings
Psalm 80:1-7. After the reading, say something like, "When I was young, I could always tell when my parents were angry with me. I could tell by the look on their faces." (Make a mean face.) Ask, "Do I make mean faces at you when I am mad?" These questions can provide an occasion for fun as well as affirmation.

Continue, "The Psalmist is talking about God being angry. God was so angry that the Psalmist could not see God's face. That is one way the Bible talks about God being near. They could not really see God's face, but they knew that God was not pleased. They felt as though God had turned his face away from them. The Psalmist wanted God with the people of Israel."

Select a poster (or all of them). Because of the birth of Jesus, we know that God is with us. We can be thankful that God does not turn away from us. God turns toward us and loves us.

Closing Prayer
Close your worship time in a few moments of silence. Ask God to forgive us for our failures and not be angry with us.

Family Journal

_____

_____

_____

_____

_____

Tuesday

Therefore the LORD . . . shall name him Immanuel.
(Isaiah 7:14)

Scripture Reading
Isaiah 7:10-16. The people of Israel were facing a tough situation. A foreign army was about to invade and take over their homes and lands. The people of Israel thought that God had left them.

The prophet Isaiah wanted the people of Israel to know God was not pleased with their actions. The prophet also wanted the people to know that God was holding them responsible for their actions. God did not stop loving Israel, however. (Refer to the posters made earlier) The prophet gave the people a vivid symbol of hope. He pointed to a young pregnant woman and said, "By the time this child is old enough to eat solid food, you will know that God is with you." To drive this message home, the prophet said the child would be named Immanuel, which means God is with us.

In time, Jesus was called Immanuel (read Matt 1:23). We have learned that because of the birth of Jesus, God is always with us.

Closing Prayer
Close your worship time in prayer. Allow family members to pray in their own words, asking God to be with us.

Family Journal

_____

_____

_____

_____

_____

Wednesday

Paul, a servant of Jesus Christ . . .
declared to be the Son of God. (Romans 1:4)

Scripture Reading
Romans 1:1-7. Begin by asking everyone to try and remember signs they have seen along the highway. Children too young too read may be encouraged to remember pictures or colors. After a few moments, show everyone the poster you made that says "Jesus is God's Son." Continue by saying, "God wanted to make sure that everyone knew that Jesus was God's Son.

How did God do that?" Read Romans 1:4 again. God declared, or literally, made a big sign that said, "Jesus is God's Son."

Because Jesus is God's Son, we are able to know God. We are also able to understand a very important lesson. God is with us all the time. God's love, protection, mercy, and forgiveness are always close at hand. If we ever doubt God's presence, all we need to do is remember to look for the big sign.

Closing Prayer
Close your worship time in prayer. Thank God for making Jesus known to us.

Family Journal

_____

_____

_____

_____

_____

_____

Thursday

God is with us. (Matthew 1:23)

Scripture Reading
Matthew 1:18-25. Repeat the exercise from Monday. Provide paper and markers and encourage family members to draw a picture or make a sign that conveys the idea that God is with us. Encourage creativity as before.

After a few moments, you might say, "God wanted us to know how much Jesus would effect our lives. To help us understand how important Jesus' life would be to us, God sent an angel to Joseph to tell him that Jesus would be called Immanuel, God with us.

"This may sound confusing. Jesus' name is Jesus. We call him Jesus, and so did his friends and family. So how can he also be Immanuel? Immanuel is not so much Jesus' name, but a term used to describe what he did for us. Because of Jesus' life, death, and resurrection, we are blessed to have God with us all the time. God is always with us in the person of Jesus."

Closing Prayer
Instruct family members to be silent for a moment and imagine Jesus standing with your family. Close in prayer. Thank God for always being with us.

Family Journal

_____

_____

_____

_____

_____

Putting Faith into Action!

Jesus makes God's presence real for everyone. We may also share in this work. It is possible for people to see and know God because of things we say and do. Think of some people who have helped you feel close to God. These persons may be ministers, teachers, doctors, or just close friends. Come up with a list. Is there one person common to the whole family? Make a colorful card or poster for this person. Thank them for helping make God's presence real in your life.

Christmas Day
Theme: Joy!

For a child has been born for us, a son given to us; authority rests upon his shoulders; and he is named Wonderful Counselor, Mighty God, Everlasting Father, Prince of Peace. (Isaiah 9:6)

Scripture Readings
Psalm 96; Isaiah 9:2-7; Titus 2:11-14; Luke 2:1-14

Use one or all of the suggested scripture readings for the celebration of Christmas Day. One workable approach is simply to read Luke 2:1-14.

Use the gifts this week (probably opened by this time) as object lessons. We give small gifts to each other. God gave the gift of life by sending Jesus into the world. This gift was made known to shepherds. The angels who made the announcement departed singing hymns of joy and praise. The proper response to the small gifts we give each other and the great gift God gives us in Jesus, is joyful gratitude. Pause and give thanks.

Putting Faith into Action!

Share the joy of the Christmas season with others today. Spend time with neglected family members. Do you know anyone spending the day alone? Do you have friends who will spend Christmas week in the hospital or nursing home. Lead your family to live out the joyful news that a Savior is born!

First Week after Christmas
Theme: Sunlight and Shadow

Scripture Readings for the Week
Psalm 148; Isaiah 63:7-9; Hebrews 2:10-18; Matthew 2:13-23

Materials Needed
You will need a large sheet of paper or poster board. Have on hand some crayons or markers. Working as a family, draw a picture of your family on a picnic. Make sure there is plenty of blue sky and sunshine. Let the children draw themselves into the picture. Have one of the adults draw a gray cloud on one corner of the poster board. If the children ask about the cloud say, "Sometimes, it even rains on picnics."

Monday

Praise the LORD! (Psalm 148:1)

Scripture Reading
Psalm 148. After the reading, say something like, "It is easy to imagine that the Psalmist just returned from a picnic at the beach. The words are all positive and joyful. This is how we should talk when our lives are in sunshine. We are happy and know that God is taking care of us. We know that our world is beautiful. Our hearts are filled with joy and thankfulness."

Invite family members to remember times when they felt this happy. (Since Christmas is just a few days passed, don't be surprised to find it mentioned.) "Let's call these happy times in our lives our Sunlight Days."

Closing Prayer
Join hands and invite family members to offer prayers in their own words. Thank God for days of joy and happiness.

Family Journal

_____

_____

_____

_____

_____

Tuesday

I will recount the gracious deeds of the LORD. (Isaiah 63:7)

Scripture Reading

Isaiah 63:7-9. After the reading, you might ask, "Was the prophet talking about a picnic?" Allow time for response. Read the passage again. Continue by saying, "The prophet was not talking about a happy experience. The people of Israel were suffering in oppression and pain. They were held captive by a powerful empire. God heard their cries, 'redeemed' them out of their prisons, and set them free. Their response is joy just like the Psalmist's joy yesterday.

"Sometimes we come into the sunlight out of the shadow of a storm (remember the dark cloud?). The sunlight is even more beautiful to us because we have stayed so long in the dark. We are thankful and happy because God brings us back to the light of happiness and joy."

Think of times in your life when things were not good, but got better. Did we remember to be thankful? Did we appreciate life more? Life is both sunlight and shadow. Therefore, we must learn to live in both.

Closing Prayer

Close in prayer. Thank God for bringing us out of the dark storms of life. Be sure to express thanksgiving for God's presence in our lives.

Family Journal

_____
_____
_____
_____
_____
_____

Wednesday

Because [Christ] was tested by what he suffered, he is able to help those who are being tested. (Hebrews 2:18)

Scripture Reading

Hebrews 2:10-18. Show the picnic picture again. Say something like, "So far we have talked about living in sunlight and how happy that makes us. We have also talked about moving out of the shadow of the storm into sunlight and how happy that makes us. Now we must talk about another part of life storms that do not go away.

"The writer of Hebrews reminds us that God offers salvation to us through the suffering of Jesus. His pain brings us life. The writer goes on to say, however, that because we are followers of Jesus, there may come a time when we will also suffer. There are in fact times in life when suffering comes and does not end happily." Allow family members an opportunity to talk about times in their lives when they experienced pain or disappointment. If a family member or friend has died, this may be an example. Even though we believe in heaven and eternal life, the death of a loved one still leaves an empty place in our lives.

If you find all this too heavy for children, you may want to relate the idea of suffering to the death of a pet. The point to make here is that life, unlike fairy tales, does not always end happily ever after. Yet, even in the midst of suffering, there is cause to give thanks. God can work through our pain to help others.

Closing Prayer

Instruct family members to be silent for a moment. Thank God for taking care of us even when the sun does not shine in our lives at all.

Family Journal

_____

_____

_____

_____

_____

Thursday

Herod is about to search for the child, to destroy him. (Matt 2:13)

Scripture Reading

Matthew 2:13-23. "Sometimes sunshine and shadow run together. The story from Matthew reflects this life situation. Baby Jesus is in danger, but an angel warns Joseph of the threat from Herod. The tiny family escapes into Egypt. This is cause for rejoicing.

"Unfortunately, the children of Bethlehem fell victim to Herod's order. Herod's soldiers blindly carry out their orders and kill all children under the age of two. A cry of pain went up from the city to the very ears of God. We wonder how something like this could happen. Jesus escapes, and that is good, but why can't the other children escape as well?"

Our own world is very similar. Look at the picture of the picnic. We enjoy so much in our world we live in the light but on the edge of the picture we have another drawing. There are people who do not picnic. They live in the shadows of poverty and pain.

"One of the reasons Jesus came into the world was to call people out of darkness and into the light. Those of us who live in the light have a responsibility to call to those in darkness. We are called to offer hope, encouragement, and even warning. Let's be sure that our picnic never blinds us to someone else's pain."

Closing Prayer

Thank God for our blessings. Pray as a family and ask God how we might use our abundance to help others.

Family Journal

_____

_____

_____

_____

_____

Putting Faith into Action!

Can you think of someone who lives under a cloud, or in the shadows of life. You may know someone who is sick or in prison or lonely. Work out a plan for bringing some sunshine into this person's life. You may provide reading material, food, or simply write a letter of encouragement. You may pay the person a visit, or call them on the phone. Try to find a way to lighten the burden in this person's life with your care and concern.

Epiphany of the Lord

Nations shall come to your light,
and kings to the brightness of your dawn. (Isaiah 60:3)

The word Epiphany means "appearance." The celebration
of Epiphany in our churches is intended to focus on the
appearance or manifestation of God in Jesus of Nazareth.

Epiphany of the Lord[4]
Theme: Calling All People

Scripture Readings for the Week
Psalm 72:1-7, 10-14; Isaiah 60:1-6; Ephesians 3:1-12; Matthew 2:1-12

Materials Needed
Take a large sheet of poster board or paper and roll it into a cone. Use it as a makeshift bull horn. We are making an announcement to different kinds of people this week that they are called to become part of God's family.

Monday

*In his days may righteousness
flourish and peace abound. (Psalm 72)*

Scripture Reading
Psalm 72:1-7, 10-14. After the reading, have some fun with the bull horn. "Calling all people, calling all people. Hear Ye, Hear Ye!" Allow children to play too! After a few minutes of play, ask, "Why would we need to use a real bull horn?" The answer you are looking for is "To help people hear what we are saying."

The psalm we read today is a prayer for the king, but it is also an announcement. The Psalmist is saying to certain people, "Hey, God is for you! God is on your side! God is working to bring fairness and justice into the world!"

When these words are voiced in a prayer for the king, it was as if they were shouted through a bull horn. Everyone would know how the king was supposed to treat people. They would also know that everyone was included in God's family. Ask family members to name someone in our world who might need an announcement like this. When we pray for our national leaders, what do we ask God to remind them to do? Who benefits from our prayers?

Closing Prayer
Allow everyone an opportunity to pray. Ask God to help our leaders care for the weak, the needy, and the poor in our land.

Family Journal

_____

_____

_____

_____

Tuesday

Arise, shine; for your light has come,
and the glory of the Lord has risen upon you.
(Isaiah 60:1)

Scripture Reading

Isaiah 60:1-6. We saw in the psalm yesterday how a prayer on behalf of the king was able to benefit others who were listening. The prophet does something similar in today's passage. The words we read today were addressed to the people of Israel in exile. The promise is that their long exile will soon end, but there are some side effects. As they return home, as the light of God's grace shines on them, people from the rest of the world will see the light and be drawn to it. Even people who have never heard of Israel's God will come to see what is happening. They will be so glad to see the light and hear the good news that they will bring gifts.

Even though the prophet aimed his words at Israel, he might as well have raised a bull horn and said, "Hey, all you people in the dark follow the light!" These words would eventually come to apply to the life and work of Jesus. Can you guess why? (Read the verses again.)

Closing Prayer

Close in your worship time in prayer. Thank God for calling us, and all people, out of darkness and into the light.

Family Journal

_____
_____
_____
_____
_____
_____

Wednesday

. . . The Gentiles have become fellow heirs, members of the same body, and sharers in the promise in Christ Jesus through the gospel. (Ephesians 3:6)

Scripture Reading

Ephesians 3:1-12. So far, we have listened to announcements that have addressed indirectly the needy and those in darkness. In our reading today, Paul makes the announcement loud and clear. . . . Gentiles have become fellow heirs . . . (v. 6).

Paul raised the bull horn and announced to the whole world, "Calling all People! Calling all people! Every promise of blessing and life made to the people of Israel is hereby offered to every person in the world. It was God's plan all along. No one is left out. Everyone is invited in."

Invite family members to think about what this means. Who in our world is left out? Who in our world is invited in? What can we do to help?

Closing Prayer

Give thanks to God for extending a call to love and fellowship to everyone, including us.

Family Journal

_____

_____

_____

_____

_____

Thursday

*Where is the child who has
been born king of the Jews? (Matthew 2:2)*

Scripture Reading

Matthew 2:1-12. We normally read this story in connection with the birth of Jesus, but the story also has great importance for the appearance of Jesus as the king (read Psalm 72:1-7, 10-14 again). When Jesus was born, he became the fulfillment of all the hopes and dreams of God. In Jesus, God offers life to everyone the people of Israel, and all other people too.

One of the things this story helps us to understand is that many people of the world are waiting and ready to receive this calling. These wise men were not Hebrew wise men. They were Gentile wise men. They saw the star, read the Hebrew Scriptures, and found the baby King. In other words, they heard God's announcement, "Calling all people . . ." and they came.

Closing Prayer

Close your worship time in prayer. Ask God to help people know that everyone is included in the invitation to life and hope that is offered in Jesus.

Family Journal

_____

_____

_____

_____

_____

Putting Faith into Action!

Plan a small party. Invite some of your close friends. Be sure to invite some people who have never been to your home before. Will they come?

First Week after Epiphany
Theme: The Beloved Son

Scripture Readings for the Week
Psalm 29; Isaiah 42:1-9; Acts 10:34-43; Matthew 3:13-17

Materials Needed
Provide markers and sheets of paper or unruled index cards. Using your driver's license as a model, allow family members to make their own ID card. They should write or draw things that identify who they are (name, address, parents name, likes, dislikes, and so on. We will add to the list as we go along).

Monday

The voice of the LORD is powerful;
the voice of the LORD is full of majesty. (Psalm 29:4)

Scripture Reading
Psalm 29. After the reading, ask something like, "What are some of the ways we recognize people?" We know people by their looks, by their smell (cologne, hopefully!), and by their actions. We also recognize people by the sound of their voice.

The Psalmist makes a strong appeal to the power of God's voice. God is known by what God says. This will become important this week. God's voice not only tells us who God is, but also who Jesus is. Have family members add to their ID cards a description of their voice.

Closing Prayer
Close in your worship time with a few moments of prayerful silence. Ask God to teach us how to listen for God's voice and to know it when we hear it.

Family Journal

_____

_____

_____

_____

_____

Tuesday

Here is my servant, whom I uphold,
my chosen, in whom my soul delights. (Isaiah 42:1)

Scripture Reading

Isaiah 42:1-9. God makes sure the people know that the message is real. Verse 8 says, "I am the Lord, that is my name . . ." God's identity here is not in doubt. The purpose of the message is not to make God known, but to make God's chosen servant known. God states what the servant is to do, and how the servant will do the work assigned to him.

God, using an unmistakable voice of authority, identified the servant as one who would bring light and life. Who is this servant? How will we recognize him? Have family members add to their ID cards descriptions of what they are supposed to do. (For instance, I am Dad. I work and help Mom with the house and yard.)

Closing Prayer

As a family, ask God to help us know the right things to do. Be sure to express thanksgiving for God's presence in our lives.

Family Journal

_____

_____

_____

_____

_____

Wednesday

We are witnesses to all that he did
both in Judea and in Jerusalem. (Acts 10:39)

Scripture Reading

Acts 10:34-43. We are partly known by the people we associate with. If we hang out with outlaws, we may be known as an outlaw. If we hang out with good people, we may be identified with them.

Peter and the other apostles made the point that they were trying to be identified with Jesus (v. 39). They wanted their lives to be shaped by the truth revealed in Jesus. Their mission in life even comes from things Jesus said and did. In fact, the word Christian actually means "little Christ," or someone who imitates Christ. Have family members add to their ID cards, "Tries to follow Jesus and learn from him how to live."

Closing Prayer

Close your worship time in prayer. Ask God to help us as we try to build our lives on Jesus' example.

Family Journal

_____
_____
_____
_____
_____
_____

Thursday

And a voice from heaven said, "This is my Son, the Beloved, with whom I am well pleased."
(Matthew 3:17)

Scripture Reading

Matthew 3:13-17. So how did Jesus know what to do? Where did he get his identity from? How did he know what God wanted him to do? These are good questions. They are all answered by our reading for today.

After Jesus was baptized, God spoke. The voice of God announced, "This is my beloved son, in whom my soul delights . . ." These words sound a lot like Isaiah 42. Jesus heard

God say, "you are the servant." Jesus knew his identity. His ID card said, "This is Jesus, the servant of God, chosen to bring justice, light, and salvation to all people."

When we are baptized, although we may not hear the voice of God, we can be sure we know what God wants. God wants us to follow Jesus as servants. Our identity is tied to his. Our baptism links our lives to his life. Have family members write on their ID cards, "Follower of Jesus."

Closing Prayer

Close in your worship time. Allow everyone an opportunity to pray. Ask God to help us as we try to pattern our lives after Jesus.

Family Journal

_____
_____
_____
_____
_____
_____

Putting Faith into Action!

We are known by what we say, by who we know, who we follow, and by what we do. We make Christ visible by our acts and words of kindness. Encourage family members to do things and say things that serve to make God's presence known to other family members. For instance, offering assistance without being asked, or serving one another at meal time. If you have extended family members nearby, you may want to extend the activity to them.

Second Week after Epiphany
Theme: Calling and Listening

Scripture Readings for the Week
Psalm 40:1-11; Isaiah 49:1-7; 1 Corinthians 1:1-9; John 1:29-42

Materials Needed
You will need to secure a telephone (unplugged from the wall).

Monday

I waited patiently for the LORD;
he inclined to me and heard my cry. (Psalm 40:1)

Scripture Reading
Psalm 40:1-11. After reading the psalm, you might say something like, "Last week we heard God speaking to Jesus at his baptism. The words of God served to make Jesus' identity clear. The same is true for us."

Show everyone the telephone. Say something like, "If we needed to talk to a friend right away, but they lived in another town, there are a couple of things we might do. First, we could sit by the phone and wait for our friend to call. We know that our friend will call sooner or later. The other thing we might do, however, is pick up the phone and call our friend. That is what the Psalmist did. The writer of this psalm wanted to hear from God, but instead of waiting for God to call, the Psalmist cried out to God. We learn from the Psalmist that when we call out to God, God hears us and cares for us."

Closing Prayer
Of course, we cannot call God on the phone. What can we do? (Allow time for responses.) Close your family time in prayer. Thank God for listening to us when we call.

Family Journal
_____
_____
_____
_____
_____
_____
_____

Tuesday

The LORD called me before I was born. (Isaiah 49:1)

Scripture Reading

Isaiah 49:1-7. Using the phone again, ask family members this question, "What do you think God would say to us if God did use the phone to call us? Would God tell us what heaven is like? Or, do think God would tell us what earth should be like?"

Read the verses in Isaiah. Continue the discussion by asking, "God called Isaiah. What was Isaiah told? What was the message? When God calls it is to teach us, direct us, or send us. Just as Jesus was given his identity at baptism, so are we. We become followers of Christ. Our task is to listen for God's call. How can we hear the call from God? God's call comes through the Scriptures, our prayers, public worship, and home worship.

"Once we hear the call we will know who we are and how we are to live. We learn our purpose in life; we learn our job. What was Isaiah's job? What was Jesus' job? What is your job?"

Closing Prayer

Close in your time of worship in prayer. Thank God for finding ways to communicate to us who we are and what we are to do with our lives.

Family Journal

_____

_____

_____

_____

_____

_____

Wednesday

. . . Called to be saints. (1 Corinthians 1:2)

Scripture Reading

1 Corinthians 1:1-9. (The word "called" occurs three times in these verses. Underline the word beforehand and exaggerate the word as you read the verses.) After the reading, hold up the telephone and say something like, "Well, judging from these verses in Corinthians, it is not just prophets that God calls. According to Paul, who gets a call from God?" (Everyone is called to receive Christ as Savior.)

"Why does God call everyone and not just special ones?" Allow time for response. "If everyone is called, does that mean that everyone is the same in God's sight? (Yes!) If everyone is called, does that mean that everyone has the same need for God's love and forgiveness? (Yes!) So if God did call us, we can guess what God would say. (Pick up the phone.) 'Hello, this is God. Listen, I want you to become part of my people. I want you to follow Jesus and listen to his teaching. I want you to have contact with other Christians. I want you to worship, study, and grow. When its time to tell you more . . . I'll call you!' "

Closing Prayer
Thank God for calling everyone to be part of God's family. Ask God to help us hear our calling.

Family Journal

_____
_____
_____
_____
_____
_____
_____

Thursday

I came baptizing with water . . .
that he might be revealed to Israel. (John 1:1:31)

Scripture Reading
John 1:29-42. Last week we learned that God spoke to Jesus during his baptism and told him who he was. Our reading today gives us another view on this event. John the Baptist pointed to Jesus as the one all people should follow. He found this out while he was doing the thing God called him to do.

This is a very important lesson. As we go through life there will be times when we wish God would call us on the phone and tell us what to do. That, of course, does not happen, but it is possible to find solutions to life's difficulties. Here is how it works: *To find out what we do not know, we must first be faithful in doing what we do know.*

We will probably never find God on the other end of the phone. We can, however, learn to listen and hear the many different ways God speaks in our world. By serving faithfully and doing what we already know to do, God will find a way to tell us and show us the rest.

Closing Prayer

Close in the worship time in prayer. Thank God for calling us into God's family. Pray that we might all learn how to live our lives in way that allows us to listen.

Family Journal

_____

_____

_____

_____

_____

_____

Putting Faith into Action!

Provide everyone a sheet of paper. If you have children too young to write, assign someone to sit with them and write down their responses. Encourage family members to come up with two lists. The first list will include those questions you would like answered. These might include "What will I be when I grow up?" or "Will I marry when I grow up?" There may also be some tough questions such as, "Why did Daddy have to leave?" or "Why did Grandpa die?" (Parents: Do not worry about trying to answer these impossible questions. It is important only for your children, and you, to be able to ask them.)

The second list will include those things that you already know about. Some of these might include, "Keeping my room clean," "Being polite to people," or "Going to Church on Sunday." This list can be long. We have many "oughts" and "shoulds" in our lives. Try to help children identify really important truths that they are already aware of.

Place the two lists side by side. Encourage everyone to post the list where they can see it everyday. Say something like, "Let's promise together as a family to do the things we already know about. If we do, God will eventually help us know about the things we don't know about. God will find a way to call us."

Third Week after Epiphany
Theme: The Light of Jesus' Ministry

Scripture Readings for the Week
Psalm 27:1, 4-9; Isaiah 9:1-4; 1 Corinthians 1:10-18; Matthew 4:12-23

Materials Needed
Gather a flashlight, candle, or lamp without a shade for use in your worship times this week.

Monday

*The LORD is my light
and my salvation, whom shall I fear? (Psalm 27:1)*

Scripture Reading
Psalm 27:1, 4-9. After the reading, allow children a few moments to enjoy the light. If you are using a flashlight, pass it around for everyone to handle. Other light, such as a candle, may be enjoyed from a safe distance. After a few moments, you might say, "Most people are fascinated by light, and we should be. Light is very important to us. Without light, we would stumble around in the dark.

"The Bible uses the idea of light to describe what God does for our lives. The Psalmist says, 'The LORD is my light and salvation.' This means that because of God's presence in our lives, we do not stumble through life. We learn how to live. We live the way God wants us to."

Ask, "What are some ways God gives us light?" (Answers may be literal, such as sun and moon. Also encourage answers such as, washing our hands, eating good food, and so on. Move gradually to other examples of light: forgiveness, kindness, generosity, prayer, worship, compassion for others, and so on. Explain how these attitudes and actions are also light.

Closing Prayer
Join hands and invite family members to offer a prayer in their own words. Thank God for being our light and salvation.

Family Journal
_____
_____
_____
_____
_____
_____
_____

Tuesday

*The people who walk in
darkness have seen a great light. (Isaiah 9:2)*

Scripture Reading

Isaiah 9:1-4. Try to make the room as dark as possible. After the reading, move the flashlight or candle around the room. Be sure to point out how the light creeps into dark places and brightens them. Continue by saying, "Yesterday we learned that the Bible uses the idea of light to describe what is good and helpful. If that is true, then what does the Bible mean by darkness? (Allow time for everyone to answer the question.) Darkness means all that is hurtful, evil, and against human life.

"The prophet addresses his words to people who walked in darkness. What do you think the verse means?" (Live in pain, suffering, oppression, and so on.) The prophet speaks to these people and assures them that the light of God is coming. When the light comes, the darkness will disappear. The people will rejoice. Ask, "How do you think God sent light to people who walked in darkness?"

Closing Prayer

Instruct family members to close their eyes and be silent for a few moments. Ask each person to thank God for the light as they open their eyes.

Family Journal

_____

_____

_____

_____

_____

_____

_____

Wednesday

*. . . Be united in the same mind
and the same purpose. (1 Corinthians 1:10)*

Scripture Reading

1 Corinthians 1:10-18. After the reading, say something like, "The word 'light' does not appear in this reading. However, Paul is encouraging his friends to live in the light. When people argue and fight, they are living in the dark. But, when people work together in unity and harmony, they live and walk in the light. The church is one place where we ought to be in the light."

Ask, "Can you think of times when you and your friends have been mad at each other? How did that make you feel? Did you feel better when you were all friends again?" Allow family member time to respond.

Closing Prayer

Close in your worship time in prayer. Ask God to help work to be in harmony with other people.

Family Journal

_____

_____

_____

_____

_____

_____

Thursday

. . . Light has dawned. (Matthew 4:16)

Scripture Reading

Matthew 4:12-23. Matthew's gospel draws all the clues together. Jesus is the light. His words and actions are aimed at moving people out of darkness into the light. His first steps are to call people to follow him in the light. His first actions are healing people in pain. Jesus came to bring people out of the darkness of suffering and into the light of hope.

Shine the flashlight around the room (or call attention to the candle burning). Say something like, "There are many people in our world trapped in one sort of darkness or another. They must wonder every day if there is any chance for them to find their way out. Jesus is the way out." Ask family members to name ways in which they came tell others of Jesus' light.

Closing Prayer

Thank God for sending Jesus as the light for those of us who sit in darkness.

Family Journal

_____

_____

_____

_____

_____

_____

Putting Faith into Action!

Review the emphasis for the week. Decide as a family whether you know someone who lives in darkness. Maybe you know someone who has recently gone through a divorce. Perhaps there is someone who has lost his or her job. The death of a spouse, parent, or child, can be a devastating time in the life of a person. Perhaps you know someone who is lonely.

After discovering whether or not you know someone who may be hurting, devise a strategy for bringing light into that person's life. You might send a handmade card, or flowers, or just a note. You may cook something for this person. Be light in their life!

Fourth Week after Epiphany
Theme: Be All That You Should Be!

Scripture Readings for the Week
Psalm 15; Micah 6:1-8; 1 Corinthians 1:18-31; Matthew 5:1-12

Materials Needed
Make a colorful poster that says, "BE ALL THAT YOU SHOULD BE!" Point out that this is not the Army slogan that says, Be all that you *can* be.

Monday

Those who do these things shall never be moved.
(Psalm 15:5)

Scripture Reading
Psalm 15. Before reading this psalm, show everyone the poster you have made. Point out that we are not talking about becoming all we can, but rather we are trying to become all we *should*. God knows how we are supposed to live. As we grow, one of our goals should be to learn to live the way God wants us to. We learn that from the Scriptures.

Now read the psalm. Encourage family members to listen for the words that describe all that we should be. After the reading, give family members an opportunity to put into their own words what they learned. Read the psalm again and repeat the discussion process. Do this until all of the items in the psalm have been discussed.

Closing Prayer
Close your worship time in prayer. Ask God to help us be all we should be.

Family Journal

_____

_____

_____

_____

_____

_____

_____

Tuesday

With what shall I come before the LORD,
and bow myself before God on high? (Micah 6:6)

Scripture Reading

Micah 6:1-8. After the reading, say something like, "The prophet Micah has set this chapter up as if God were suing his people for bad behavior. God calls the mountains and the foundations of the world as witnesses. God makes this point: 'I've been all that I should be for you, but you have not been all you should be for me.' "

In verse 6, the prophet asks the question that all of us want to know. What does God require? What does God want from me? The answer is given in verse 8. To be all we should be, God requires that we:

1. ***Do justice.*** That means treat people fairly.
2. ***Love kindness.*** That means to treat people with love and compassion, working for the well being of others.
3. ***Walk humbly with God.*** That means that we do not take our relationship with God as something we deserve or neglect.

To walk with God means to walk as God walks. In other words to be all we should be!

Closing Prayer

Give thanks to God for being willing to walk with us. Thank God for being all that God should be for us. Ask for help in becoming all that you *should* be for God.

Family Journal

_____
_____
_____
_____
_____
_____
_____

Wednesday

God chose what is weak . . . so that no one
might boast in the presence of God.
(1 Corinthians 1:27-29)

Scripture Reading

1 Corinthians 1:18-31. After the reading, say something like, "If we are going to be all we should be, one the things we must admit is that we are weak. We can get sick, we can get hurt, we bruise, and we can even die. If we are not careful, we will forget we are weak. If we do forget, we will end up acting as though we are strong, tough, and even indestructible. That is not the way we are, however, and not the way we should be."

Call on family members to give examples of how we are weak. After a few moments, call for examples of how we act tough and strong. Continue by saying, "You see, if we can learn to live with our weaknesses, then we can be helpful and understanding to other people with weaknesses. If we act strong and tough all the time, however, we might forget how it feels to be hurt. We might even hurt someone else.

"Paul says that the cross of Jesus is all about weakness. Since we are weak anyway, we shouldn't have any problem accepting who we are."

Closing Prayer
Close in your worship time in prayer. Thank God for understanding our weakness and for meeting us where we are. Ask God to help us understand the weakness of others and meet them where they are.

Family Journal

_____
_____
_____
_____
_____
_____
_____

Thursday

Blessed are you . . . (Matthew 5:11)

Scripture Reading
Matthew 5:1-12. After the reading, say something like, "These verses are usually called 'The Beatitudes.' The word 'beatitude' means 'that which makes us happy.' The idea is that if we do these things, we will live the kind of life God intends, and we will be happy and fulfilled."

Taken together, these beatitudes are a list of all that we should be.

Poor in spirit means not thinking more highly of ourselves than we should.

Mourning means not being afraid to look at the pain and suffering in the world.

Meekness means a disciplined life.

Righteousness means right relationships between people.

Showing mercy means giving people a chance to make their lives better.

Pure in heart means that we do not try to be something we are not.

Peacemakers work to bring an end to violence, anger, and conflict in our world.

"These words are the heart of Jesus' message to us. They are a quick capsule of all that we should be. Some of these are hard, but all of them are important. Together these attitudes will form in us a life that is worth living and enjoyable."

Closing Prayer
Thank God for giving us the list of beatitudes. Ask God to help each family member to live out the beatitudes this week.

Family Journal

_____
_____
_____
_____
_____
_____

Putting Faith into Action!

Encourage family members to identify one of the Beatitudes that they believe they would like to have in their life. Parents should take the lead here. Promise one another that you will work everyday to become all you should be. Have everyone promise to help each other through this process.

Fifth Week after Epiphany
Theme: You are Salt!

Scripture Readings for the Week
Psalm 112:1-10; Isaiah 58:1-12; 1 Corinthians 2:1-12; Matthew 5:13-20

Materials Needed
You will need water and a tablespoon of salt. (On Wednesday, you will need a tablespoon of sugar).

Monday

For the righteous will never be moved;
they will be remembered forever. (Psalm 112:6)

Scripture Reading
Psalm 112:1-10. After the reading, take the glass of water and pass it around. Tell everyone to take a sip. After the glass has been around, stir in the tablespoon of salt. Pass the glass around again. You might ask something like, "How is the water different? How could such a small amount of salt make such a big difference in so much water?"

The Psalmist described how God's people made a difference in the world. Read the psalm again. Have family members listen for all the ways the people of God made their presence known. You might say something like, "If we live the way we are supposed to, our lives can make a huge impact on our community and our world, just like salt in water."

Closing Prayer
Close in your worship time in prayer. Ask God to help us live lives that make our world a better place. Be sure to express thanksgiving for God's presence in our lives.

Family Journal

_____

_____

_____

_____

_____

_____

_____

Tuesday

Is not this the fast that I choose: to loose the bonds of injustice . . . and to break every yoke? (Isaiah 58:6)

Scripture Reading

Isaiah 58:1-12. Remind everyone what happened with the water yesterday. Ask, "How did the salt make the water salty?" (Affirm all responses.) The simple answer to this question is this: The salt changes the water simply by being itself. Salt makes things salty!

In the same way, the prophet Isaiah told the people of Israel how to be a real community. It is not by elaborate worship exercises (fasting and sacrifice). Rather, the way to have a community is to *be* the community. This is done by feeding the hungry, caring for the weak, and encouraging the discouraged.

The message is so simple we sometimes miss it. The best way to make our community a place where people feel welcome and safe is by helping people feel welcome and safe.

Closing Prayer

Close in your worship time in prayer. Allow everyone an opportunity to pray. Ask God to help us live in peace with other people.

Family Journal

_____
_____
_____
_____
_____
_____

Wednesday

For I decided to know nothing among you except Jesus Christ, and him crucified. (1 Corinthians 2:2)

Scripture Reading

1 Corinthians 2:1-12. Fill the glass with water, but this time add a table spoon of sugar. Pass the glass around and allow everyone to comment on the difference. After everyone has noticed the difference (hopefully), you might say something like, "Only salt tastes like salt. Sugar may look like salt from a distance, but once we taste it there can be no doubt.

"That is what Paul meant when he talked about wisdom of the world and God's wisdom. There are lots of ideas that sound good, or look good from a distance, but there is only one truth. That truth is found in Jesus Christ. The best way we have of helping others find this truth is just talk about it in plain terms."

Closing Prayer

Close your worship time together. Ask God to help us live and speak the truth about Jesus plainly. If we do, then people will always know where true life can be found.

Family Journal

_____

_____

_____

_____

_____

Thursday

You are the salt of the earth. (Matthew 5:13)

Scripture Reading

Matthew 5:13-20. Read Jesus' words carefully. He did not say we should be salt, nor did he say that we ought to be salt. He did not even command us, "Be Salt!" Instead, Jesus said simply that we are the salt of the earth. What does that mean?

If we are the salt, then we are the only salt. We are the only ones who can do what salt does. In the ancient world, salt was used to make things clean. Salt also preserved food and added flavor. These are the things we are to do: preserve, cleanse, and flavor!

Pass the water around. As the glass goes around, say something like, "Pretend this water was full of terrible germs, germs that could kill or makes us sick. Pretend that the only thing that will clean the water is salt. If all that was true, we would want to be sure that the salt was there before we tried to drink the water. Well, Jesus said, 'You are the salt of the earth.' That is who we are. Our job is to make the world salty, to make a difference."

Closing Prayer

Join hands and invite family members to pray in their own words. Ask God to help us salt our world and make it better.

Family Journal

_____

_____

_____

_____

_____

Putting Faith into Action!

Take a look around your community. Do you see anything that needs doing? Maybe there is trash on the ground in the park? Maybe the windows of an elderly person need cleaning. Volunteers are often needed at the local shelter. Find something that needs your salt, and salt it!

Sixth Week after Epiphany[5]
Theme: Walking With God

Scripture Readings for the Week
Psalm 119:1-8; Deuteronomy 30:15-20; 1 Corinthians 3:1-9; Matthew 5:21-37

Materials Needed
Play follow the leader. Be sure you make the rules clear. Each person must do everything the leader does.

Monday

I will praise you with an upright heart,
when I learn your righteous ordinances. (Psalm 119:7)

Scripture Reading
Psalm 119:1-8. Read the psalm after playing follow the leader. After the reading, you might say something like, "Following God is a lot like the game we played. God is the leader. God knows the way we should go. By watching closely and listening carefully, we can follow God and live the kind of life we should. Following God means following instructions."

Read the psalm again. Invite family members to respond to this question, "What did the

Psalmist say will happen if we carefully walk the way God wants us to?" Allow time to respond.

Closing Prayer
Close in your time of worship in prayer. Ask God to teach us to walk as God walks.

Family Journal

_____

_____

_____

_____

_____

Tuesday

See, I have set before you today life and
prosperity, death and adversity. (Deuteronomy 30:15)

Scripture Reading
Deuteronomy 30:15-20. Play follow the leader again. Let your hair down and have some fun. After playing for a while, read the verses from Deuteronomy. After the reading, you might say

something like, "Playing follow the leader is fun. If we make a mistake, we can just laugh about it. Following God's teachings, however, is not a game. Mistakes can be painful."

Illustrate this for children by asking, "What are some of the rules that our family has that are intended to protect us and keep us safe? (These might include staying out of the street, not talking to strangers, coming straight home from school, and so on.) God's commandments and teaching are the same way. They are to help us live and be happy. We follow God, and keep the rules, and God leads us in ways that are good for us. If we don't follow, we might wander off into something not good for us."

Closing Prayer
Ask God to help us learn the how to follow and listen carefully to the things God teaches us. Be sure to express thanksgiving for God's presence in our lives.

Family Journal
_____
_____
_____
_____
_____
_____
_____

Wednesday

And so, brothers and sisters, I could not speak to you as spiritual people, but rather . . . as infants in Christ.
(1 Corinthians 3:1)

Scripture Reading
1 Corinthians 3:1-9. Play follow the leader again. After you finish, you might ask something like, "Does it seem funny to see grown-ups playing a children's game?" Allow time for discussion. Move the discussion toward the topic of grown-up versus childish behavior. Ask for examples. Make a distinction between child-like (adults playing follow the leader,) and child-ish (stubborn refusal to do what is right).

Read the verses from 1 Corinthians. Continue by saying, "Paul told his friends that he wanted to teach them more, but they were not grown up enough, they were acting like children. One of the things we learn as we try to walk the way God wants us to is that God never runs out of things to teach us. As long as we follow, God will keep leading us. If we act child-ish and stop following God, we will stop learning and growing."

Closing Prayer
Close your time of worship in a few moments of silence. Thank God for loving us as children. Ask God to help us to be child-like without being child-ish.

Family Journal

_____
_____
_____
_____
_____
_____
_____

Thursday

You have heard that it was said
. . . But I say to you. (Matthew 5:27-28)

Scripture Reading

Matthew 5:21-32. Play the game again, but a little differently. This time, instead of moving around the room, sit on the floor and have everyone think the same thing. Say something like, "Think about a blue elephant! and so on."

After a several minutes of play you might say, "It's hard to play follow the leader in our thoughts, isn't it? Jesus, however, tells us that our thoughts are as important as our actions." Read Matthew 5:21-32.

"Anger, Jesus said, is as bad as murder. So if we want to walk the way God walks, we must also learn to think the way God thinks. Besides, our thoughts come first, and our actions follow. God wants us to think and walk like Jesus."

Closing Prayer

Close in your time of worship in prayer. Ask God to help us think and walk in the right way.

Family Journal

_____
_____
_____
_____
_____
_____

Putting Faith into Action!

Sometimes we get mad at people and stay mad for a long time. Have everyone think real hard. Is there anyone they are mad at? This would be a good time to forgive the person. Don't think any bad thoughts about the person. Think of something nice you can do for this person, then do it.

Seventh Week after Epiphany[6]
Theme: Seeing the World God's Way

Scripture Readings for the Week
Psalm 119:33-40; Leviticus 19:1-2, 9-18; 1 Corinthians 3:10-11, 16-23; Matthew 5:38-48

Materials Needed
Use something that improves vision eye glasses, microscope, binoculars, telescope, microscope any one of these will work.

Monday *Start Here* 1/29

Teach me, O LORD, the way of your statutes, and I will observe it to the end. (Psalm 119:33)

Scripture Reading
Psalm 119:33-40. Demonstrate the object you have selected and explain how it improves vision. (Eye glasses correct impaired vision, a telescope magnifies large objects at great distances.)

After explaining the object, read the passage for today. Encourage family members to listen for words that deal with sight (observe, eyes, and so on). The Psalmist believed that God's instructions were like eye glasses (or whatever you have chosen). These instructions improve our ability to see. As we are able to see our world and our lives better, we are able to live better. We are able to live the way God wants us to live.

What are the instructions God has given us? Where do we find them? Encourage family members to spend time reflecting on these questions and be ready to discuss them tomorrow.

Closing Prayer
Close your worship time in prayer. Allow everyone an opportunity to pray. Ask God to help us see the truth in the instructions God has given us.

Family Journal
_____
_____
_____
_____
_____
_____
_____

Tuesday

You shall be holy, for I the LORD your God am holy.
(Leviticus 19:2)

Scripture Reading

Leviticus 19:1-2, 9-18. As you begin this worship time, you might say something like, "Yesterday we learned that God's instructions were like glasses they allowed us to see things more clearly. When we stopped, we were asking where those instructions are found."

Read the verses from Leviticus. Continue by saying, "These instructions are not here to teach us what we must do to make God love us. These words are here because God already loves us. The instructions help us to live good lives. How do they do that? The instructions help us to see the world the way God sees it."

Use some of the verses to illustrate this point. For example, you might say, "Verse 9 says that if we are farmers, we should leave some of our crop for poor people. We might see the farm as ours. We don't want to leave anything in the field because we want it all for ourselves. God, however, wants us to see the poor in the world and care for them. If we leave some food in the field, they can eat." Isolate other verses. See if family members can identify God's view of the world in each instance. Help children by using examples they can understand. (Verse 15, for example. Children readily understand unfairness, just try to cheat at checkers!)

Closing Prayer

Join hands and invite family members to pray in their own words. Thank God for helping us see the world in a different and better way.

Family Journal

_____
_____
_____
_____
_____
_____

Wednesday

For the wisdom of this world
is foolishness with God. (1 Corinthians 3:19)

Scripture Reading

1 Corinthians 3:10-11, 16-23. After the reading, you might say something like, "If we can't see clearly, it can be dangerous. Having good vision is important. They same is true when it comes to seeing the world the way it really is. If you see people as more important than they really are, they might hurt you or trick you. If we see people as less important than they really are, we might hurt them.

"Paul was thinking about this very problem in the verses we read today. He wanted us to beware of the wisdom of the world. The wisdom of the world means the way the world looks at things. For example, what does the world think of homeless people? (Not very important or powerful.) How does the world see rich people? (Powerful and important.)

"Paul said that Christians must see the world differently. Even if the world thinks we are foolish. The foolishness of God (that is, the way God sees things) is wiser and better than the wisdom of the world (the way the world sees things)."

Closing Prayer

Close your time together in prayer. Ask God to help us see the world the way God sees it.

Family Journal

_____

_____

_____

_____

_____

_____

Thursday

Be perfect, therefore, as your heavenly Father is perfect. (Matthew 5:48)

Scripture Reading

Matthew 5:38-48. After the reading, say something like, "The teaching of Jesus provides us some important examples of looking at the world. Notice how he begins: 'You have heard it said . . .' (v. 38). This is the way the world looks at things, but the world needs glasses!"

The world says take revenge when you need to.

God says, don't revenge.

The world says if someone hits you, hit them back.

God says, don't hit back.

The world says love your neighbors, but hate your enemies.

God says love your enemies.

"Jesus provides us with a new way to view the world. As we learn to see the world differently, we will be able to live the way God wants us to live. The world may laugh at us and say we are foolish, but God will call us wise!"

Closing Prayer

Close your worship time with a few moments of prayerful silence. Ask God to correct our vision, open our eyes, and allow us to see what needs to be done and how we might help.

Family Journal

_____

_____

_____

_____

_____

_____

_____

Putting Faith into Action!

Make a list of everyone your family knows by name. Include friends, co-workers, classmates, and extended family members. The list will be long. Most people are surprised to learn how many people they know. After the list is complete, review every name, asking this question: How does the world view this person? If you have persons on the list that the world may have labeled in some way (alcoholic, divorced, homosexual, liberal, incompetent, and so on) stop and pray for that person. Is it possible to view them in another way?

Select one or two of these persons for some sort of family project. You may prepare them a meal or send them a card. Are they welcome in your home? Why or why not?

Eighth Week after Epiphany[7]
Theme: Establishing Priorities in Life

Scripture Readings for the Week
Psalm 131; Isaiah 49:8-16a; 1 Corinthians 4:1-5; Matthew 6:24-34

Materials Needed
Cut out numerals ranging from 1 to 10, using any form of paper product found in the home.

Monday

But I have calmed and quieted my soul. (Psalm 131:2)

Scripture Reading
Psalm 131. Spread the numbers you have cut out on the floor. Working as a family, arrange the numbers in the correct order. After you are finished, read Psalm 131. Continue by saying something like, "Getting things in their right order is important. It is important for counting, such as our numbers here. It is also important in our lives. If we get the wrong thing at the beginning, we might end up in the wrong place at the end.

"The Psalmist said, 'I do not occupy myself with things too great and too marvelous for me.'

This simply means that the Psalmist had arranged life according to certain priorities. First things first, second things second, and so on. What is too much for the Psalmist to deal with is left for God to deal with."

Closing Prayer
Close your worship time in prayer. Ask God to help us arrange our lives so that the most important things are first and other things, less important things, or things we can't control, do not get in our way.

Family Journal

_____

_____

_____

_____

_____

_____

Tuesday

Even these will forget, yet I will not forget you.
(Isaiah 49:15)

Scripture Reading

Isaiah 49:8-16. Spread the numbers out on the floor. Leave out two of the numbers. Work as a family to arrange the numbers in order. Leave blank spaces for the missing numbers.

Read the verses from Isaiah. Say something like, "When we tried to arrange the numbers and some of them were missing, how did that make you feel?" Allow everyone a chance to answer. Continue by saying, "That is how people feel when they suffer and deal with pain. It is like trying to arrange numbers with some of the numbers missing.

"Isaiah's friends thought God was missing (read v. 14). Their pain and disappointment was so great they thought God had left them, but Isaiah promised them that God had not left them. God would meet them in their pain and bring them back to safety. Sometimes it is hard to arrange life in the right order. Sometimes some of the pieces are missing. When those times come, God simply asks that we do our best to get things in order. God will eventually furnish us with the missing pieces."

Closing Prayer

Thank God for caring for us even when life is hard or doesn't make sense. Be sure to express thanksgiving for God's presence in our lives.

Family Journal

_____
_____
_____
_____
_____
_____
_____

Wednesday

Moreover, it is required of stewards
that they be found trustworthy. (1 Corinthians 4:2)

Scripture Reading

1 Corinthians 4:1-5. Begin your worship time by saying something like, "I'm in charge of the number exercise today." Arrange the numbers in several different ways. First, in proper sequential order. Then, arrange the numbers in reverse order. Arrange the numbers by even and odd numbers. Finally, jumble the numbers up in no apparent order.

Read 1 Corinthians 4:1-5. Call attention to verse 2. Continue by saying something like, "It is not enough to just order our lives in any old way; God wants us to put first things first. If we know what is first and don't put it first, then we are not trustworthy." Invite members to give examples. (For instance, if I know I am supposed to pay the bills on the first of the month and wait until the tenth, I am not trustworthy. If we make promises to our friends and then don't keep those promises, we are not trustworthy.) It is not enough just to know what comes first. We must also put first, in our lives and actions, what comes first.

Closing Prayer

Close your worship time in prayer. Thank God for helping put first things first. Ask God for the grace to be more trustworthy.

Family Journal

_____
_____
_____
_____
_____
_____
_____

Thursday

But strive first for the kingdom of God . . .
and all these things will be given to you as well.
(Matthew 6:33)

Scripture Reading

Matthew 6:24-34. Spread the numbers out on the floor. Read the passage from Matthew. As you talk about the passage, pick up the numbers and place them in order.

Begin by saying, "There are many things we must do in life. (Pick up the 9 and 10). We have to eat and wear clothes, bathe and brush our teeth (pick up 7 and 8), obey the law and live as responsible people (5 and 6). We must also take care of people who are weak and in need (3 and 4), and love each other (pick up the 2). Most of all, we must seek to have God in our lives (pick up the 1)."

Read Matthew 6:33. Continue by saying, "Jesus said, that if we get the first thing right, then all the other things will fall into place." Ask, "What does Jesus say is the first thing?"

Closing Prayer

Close your worship time in prayer. Ask God to help us always to choose to do the first thing first.

Family Journal

_____
_____
_____
_____
_____
_____
_____

Putting Faith into Action!

Provide everyone with a sheet of paper and pencil or marker. Make a family "To Do List." List all the things that your family needs to do. Write down who is responsible for each thing. Arrange the items in order of importance and what day they should be done (some will be done everyday). After the list is finished, make sure that serving God is at the top of everyone's list. Post the list where everyone can see it. Agree as a family to try to do the things on the list in a trustworthy manner.

Notes

[1]Advent begins four full weeks before Christmas. After determining the first Sunday in Advent, simply back up to the preceding Monday. That is our starting point.

[2]The second week of Advent usually falls between December 4 and December 10. Begin your family worship celebration for this week on the Monday immediately following the First Sunday in Advent.

[3]The Third Sunday of Advent falls between December 11 and 17. This week's worship celebration begins on the Monday after the Second Sunday in Advent.

[4]Epiphany is celebrated January 6. Remember you are a week ahead of the calendar and are preparing for the celebration of worship in your church.

[5]Epiphany closes with beginning of Lent on Ash Wednesday. Ash Wednesday does not occur on the same date each year because it is tied to Easter. Easter is tied to the Spring equinox. Consult your calendar or church bulletin for the date of Ash Wednesday. This week could include Ash Wednesday. If it does, move ahead to the worship activities for Lent.

[6]See note for last week.

[7]See note on Sixth Week After Epiphany.

Transfiguration[1]
Theme: How God Changes Things

Scripture Readings for the Week
Psalm 2; Exodus 24:12-18; 2 Peter 1:16-21; Matthew 17:1-9

Materials Needed
Use a clear plastic cup with water. Later we will turn the mixture into ice and steam.

Monday

Today I have begotten you (Psalm 2:7)

Scripture Reading
Psalm 2. You will need a cup of water in a clear plastic container. After the reading, you might say something like, "This psalm was used in Israel when a new king began to serve. The Israelites believed the king was able to serve because God had chosen him."

Read verse 7. This verse means: "Yesterday you were not the king, but because I am God, today you are the king." Use the plastic cup and water. Imagine this cup is the king. The water is the presence of God. Without the water, it is just a plastic cup; but with the water, it is a special cup. That is the way the people saw the king.

Closing Prayer
Pass the cup around and invite everyone to take a sip. Thank God for being present with us and in us.

Family Journal
_____
_____
_____
_____
_____
_____
_____

Tuesday

The glory of the LORD . . . (Exodus 24:16)

Scripture Reading
Exodus 24:12-18. Begin by pouring the water out of the plastic cup into a small saucepan. Heat until the water begins to boil. Note the steam as it rises. After allowing everyone to watch the steam rise, read the scripture passage from Exodus.

Continue by saying, "Yesterday we talked about how God filled the king of Israel with the Spirit like water into a cup. Today we hear about Moses on a mountain receiving the law and commandments from God. The mountain was covered in a thick mist. This mist is also a picture of the presence of God.

"God can fill our world in the same way that God filled the life of an earthly king. God may speak through a thick mist, like steam rising from a boiling pot of water. God may use different ways to reach us, but it is the same God, and it is the same message."

Closing Prayer
Close your worship time in prayer. Thank God for helping us in so many ways. Thank God also for making the effort to reach out to us.

Family Journal
_____
_____
_____
_____
_____
_____
_____

Wednesday
You will do well to be attentive. (1 Peter 1:19)

Scripture Reading
2 Peter 1:16-21. Fill the cup with water well in advance of this worship time. Put the cup of water in the freezer and let the water freeze. (If you forget, just place a couple of ice cubes in the cup.)

After reading the scripture passage, pass the cup around for everyone to view. You might begin by saying something like, "The water that we saw as a liquid on Monday and as steam yesterday is now hard, frozen solid.

"God's presence can be solid as well. The writer of 2 Peter was talking about the message of God's love and grace. This message, said the writer, is fully confirmed. By this Peter meant that the message was witnessed and experienced by so many as to be beyond doubt.

"For the people of Israel it may have looked like a heavy mist on the mountain. For many early Christians, though, God was fully known and real in the person Jesus of Nazareth. Just as water can take many forms, so can God."

Closing Prayer
Allow everyone an opportunity to pray. Ask God to be present in our lives.

Family Journal

_____

_____

_____

_____

_____

_____

_____

Thursday

Lord, it is good for us to be here. (Matt 17:4)

Scripture Reading

Matthew 17:1-9. Begin with the cup of frozen water. After the reading you might say, "In Jesus, God came to us as a flesh and blood person. God was fully present in Jesus' life. In our reading for today, Jesus makes known to his disciples and us just how close God is to us.

"On the mountain, Jesus' physical appearance was changed into a glowing, heavenly being. Just like ice can change into water, and water into steam, Jesus changed before the eyes of his followers. What is the message for us? God says we are to listen to Jesus. The one who was changed on the mountain also has the power to change us."

Closing Prayer

Close your worship time with prayer. Pray for things that may need changing in our lives.

Encourage each person to share their own needs. Remember, God can change us.

Family Journal

_____

_____

_____

_____

_____

_____

Putting Faith into Action!

Everyone prayed for some kind of change. Today begin a plan to make the change happen. Parents, if your plan was to quit smoking or lose weight, tell the family how you plan to bring that change about. How do you think God will help you? Maybe your prayer was for better grades. What is your plan? How can God help? Maybe your prayer was for a better relationship with a brother or sister. What is the plan? How will God help? Don't leave this as something we just talk about. Take positive steps to bring about positive results in life. God will help us.

Lent

Create in me a clean heart, O God,
and put a new and right spirit within me. (Psalm 51:10)

The focus of Lent is "penitence," which means feeling sorry for sin or wrongdoing. The season of Lent was established by early church leaders to help Christians prepare for Jesus' suffering during Holy Week and the celebration of his Resurrection on Easter.

First Week of Lent
Theme: Living the Truth

Scripture Readings for the Week
Psalm 51:1-17; Isaiah 58:1-12; 2 Corinthians 5:20b 6:10; Matthew 6:1-6, 16-21

Materials Needed
Make up a game called "True or False." During the week family members will tell stories about something that has happened in their life. Stories may be funny or sad, true or false. The other family members must guess whether or not the story is true. Adults should start the game to get things moving. Have fun. The point is not to teach children that lying is fun, but to demonstrate that the truth about our lives is always obvious to God.

Monday 2/19

Create in me a clean heart, O God. (Psalm 51:10)

Scripture Reading
Psalm 51:1-17. Play the story game with family members. After having fun with the game, read the psalm for today.

Continue by saying something like, "It is fun to tell stories and even to make up things just for fun, but we should never make up things and try to make people believe them. That is lying, and lying is not a good thing.

"The Psalmist reminds us that it is impossible to lie to God. God knows everything. God knows what is true and what is false. The best thing we can do is always to tell God the truth."

Closing Prayer
Close your worship time in a few moments of silence. Thank God for caring enough about us to listen to what we say. Ask God to help us always to be willing to be truthful with God.

Family Journal

_____
_____
_____
_____
_____
_____

Tuesday

Look, you serve your own interest. (Isaiah 58:3b)

Scripture Reading

Isaiah 58:1-12. (These verses from Isaiah were used in the fifth week of Epiphany. Our emphasis there was on Light. The focus here is on true and false worship.)

Play the "True or False" game again. Have fun with this by making some of the stories outrageous. After a few moments of play, read the verses from Isaiah.

Continue by saying something like, "Playing games and telling stories can be fun, but if the reason for our stories is to fool, or hurt someone, then it is not fun. If playing a game keeps us from doing important things, then the game is not good. That is what the prophet Isaiah was saying to the people of Israel in these verses. He accused them of playing games at worship, of pretending. Instead of really talking to God and caring about God's people, they were just dressing up and playing worship. Playing at worship is the same thing as lying to God."

Ask, "How is playing at worship the same as lying to God?" Allow time for responses. You may want to say, "If you tell me you are cleaning your room, and you go into your room and make noises that you think will fool me, but you are really not cleaning your room at all. That is the same thing as a lie."

Closing Prayer

Close your worship time in prayer. Ask God to help us not to pretend in worship. Ask God to help us as we really try to live and tell the truth.

Family Journal

_____
_____
_____
_____
_____
_____

Wednesday

God is making his appeal through us. (2 Cor 5:20)

Scripture Reading

2 Corinthians 5:20b 6:10. Play the game "True or False." After a few moments of play, ask, "Does this game hurt anyone?" (No. Just playing a game, even if we don't tell the truth in our story, does not hurt anyone.) Continue, "Suppose we continue to tell stories that are not true. Suppose we tell them at school or work. Can that hurt anyone?" (Yes.)

Read the verses from 2 Corinthians. You might explain the verses in this way: "Paul encouraged his friends in Corinth to take seriously how the world viewed them because they were God's ambassadors. People learn about God by watching and listening to them.

"Paul then gave a long list of things that he had done in his life to help people believe in God." (Read the list in 6:3-10. Note especially verse 7.)

Continue by saying, "Paul encouraged his friends to live lives of honesty and compassion. If we care about people and are honest with our speech and lives, God may be able to touch other people through us but only if we are truthful."

Closing Prayer

Join hands and invite family members to pray in their own words. Ask God to help us live lives that help other people see God.

Family Journal

_____
_____
_____
_____
_____
_____

Thursday

. . . And your Father who sees in secret will reward you. (Matt 6:4, 6, &18)

Scripture Reading

Matthew 6:1-6, 16-21. Begin by saying, "We must talk about one more part of the 'True or False' game. Read the verses from Matthew. Call attention to the word hypocrite. Continue by saying, The word 'hypocrite' literally means 'someone who wears a mask.' A person who wears a mask is usually trying to hide something. Jesus leads us to believe that 'hypocrites' try to hide the truth about what they want.

"Jesus said, that when these people pray, it is not because they want God to hear them, but because they want other people to hear them and admire them. When they help the needy, it is not because they care about the needy, but because they want people to see them care about the needy and say nice things about them. Here is a hard lesson to learn: Even when we are doing good things, such as praying and helping the poor, we can be pretending. God does not want us to pretend. God wants us to pray because we love God, and God wants us to help the needy because we love people."

Closing Prayer

Lead your family in a time of prayerful silence. Ask God to help us do good things for the right reasons.

Family Journal

_____

_____

_____

_____

_____

_____

_____

Putting Faith into Action!

After playing the "True or False" game all week, now it is time to do the truth. Spend some time talking seriously about the things your family does for God. List them if necessary. Ask about each and every item, Why do we do this? Who are we trying to please or impress?

After the list is complete, work together as a family to make sure that all things we do for God, including this daily worship activity, are done for the right reasons so are lives will be true and not false.

Second Week of Lent
Theme: Sin and Forgiveness

Scripture Readings for the Week
Psalm 32; Genesis 2:15-17; 3:1-7; Romans 5:12-19;
Matthew 4:1-11

Materials Needed
Secure two or three liter plastic bottles half filled with soda pop. This should be the kind of bottle that has the twist on/off top.

Monday

Happy are those whose transgression is forgiven.
(Psalm 32:1)

Scripture Reading
Psalm 32. After the reading, ask family members to define sin. What is sin? How do we sin against God? Allow everyone a chance to answer. Explain sin in your own words and in a way that is consistent with your beliefs. The traditional view is that sin is any action or attitude that is contrary to the will of God.

After the discussion about sin, show everyone the bottle of soda pop. Continue by saying, "When we do things that we know are wrong, a kind of pressure builds up inside of us. This pressure is called guilt. (Give the bottle a good shake.) When we admit our sin to God, God forgives us. In other words, God relieves the guilt pressure and sets us free. (Slowly turn the cap allowing the trapped air to escape.) Just like opening this cap lets the air out, forgiveness lets the guilt out. That is what the Psalmist was writing about (read verse 1 again)."

Closing Prayer
Close your time of worship in prayer. Thank God for giving us a way to find forgiveness and release for our sin and guilt.

Family Journal
_____
_____
_____
_____
_____
_____
_____

Tuesday

Then the eyes of both were opened. (Genesis 3:7)

Scripture Reading

Genesis 2:15-17; 3:1-7. After the reading, ask family members to answer these questions: Why do we sin? Why do we do things we know we are not supposed to do? Explain that people have asked since the beginning of time. The story in our Genesis reading offers some clues.

We should not make the story say what it does not say. The story does not say that the serpent tempted Adam and Eve. They were tempted by the forbidden fruit. The serpent only gave voice to their thoughts. If we are not careful, we can tell the story in such a way that we are not responsible for our actions. The essence of sin is that we knowingly do the wrong thing.

After telling the story, introduce the soda pop bottle again. Give it a hard shake. Slowly open the cap and let the air escape. Continue by saying, "No matter how we sin or why, the result is the same. We are filled with guilt. The forgiveness of God sets us free."

Closing Prayer

Close your worship time in prayer. Ask God to help us struggle against the temptation to do what we know is wrong.

Family Journal

_____
_____
_____
_____
_____
_____

Wednesday

But the free gift is not like the trespass. (Romans 5:15)

Scripture Reading

Romans 5:12-19. After the reading, begin by saying, "We have a pretty good idea of how we sin. But how does God forgive us and why? The answer to these questions is found in our reading today." Read 5:15 again. "We all sin the way Adam and Eve did. Every person who has ever lived has sinned in similar ways, but God is not willing to leave us trapped in our guilt. Jesus came into the world to free us both from the guilt of sin and the power of sin. Jesus wants to set us free from what we have already done (the soda pop bottle) but also help us be smart enough and strong enough not to make the same mistakes again.

"Our part is to let God forgive us by allowing Jesus to open the cap and release the pressure. We do that when we allow Jesus into our lives and trust him completely."

Closing Prayer

Give thanks to God for providing a way for us to be free from the effects of our sin. Be sure to express thanksgiving for God's presence in our lives.

Family Journal

_____
_____
_____
_____
_____
_____
_____

Thursday

Worship the Lord your God. (Matthew 4:10)

Scripture Reading

Matthew 4:1-11. Before the reading, ask family members this question. How can Jesus help us as we struggle to do what is right? How can Jesus help us resist temptations to do things that we know we should not do? Allow a brief time for discussion. If children pick up on the temptation of Jesus, affirm their insight. Read the material from Matthew 4:1-11.

Continue by saying, "Jesus was tempted to do things he knew was wrong. In that way, he was just like us. Yet, Jesus did not give in. Because of this, we are encouraged to believe that we also can be faithful. If we are devoted to following Jesus, we may have the power to resist temptations to do wrong things."

Closing Prayer

Close your worship time in prayer. Ask God to help us resist the temptation to do things that we know are wrong. Thank God for allowing Jesus to be our teacher and helper in this struggle.

Family Journal

_____
_____
_____
_____
_____
_____
_____

Putting Faith into Action!

We have intentionally avoided any direct instruction to seek forgiveness this week. The discussions and object lessons may have raised family members' awareness about sin, failure, and guilt. Spend a few moments talking about the things we have learned this week. Invite family members to talk about failure in life. Parents may take the lead here. They may even need to ask forgiveness from children. Affirm the efforts of children to deal with this. (Younger children may have difficulty because of an undeveloped sense of right and wrong. Enjoy this moment of innocence!) Gradually move the discussion from sin to forgiveness. You may want to use the soda pop bottle once more. Offer forgiveness to one another for wrongs done within the family. Make plans to seek forgiveness from those outside the family who may have been wronged in some way. Finally, seek the forgiveness of God by simply asking to be forgiven.

The Third Week of Lent
Theme: God Can Change Us

Scripture Readings for the Week
Psalm 121; Genesis 12:1-4a; Romans 4:1-5, 13-17; John 3:1-17

Materials Needed
If you garden and have some flower bulbs, plan to use them. Include some flowers in full bloom, and some buds if available (Lent usually falls in early Spring). If these are not available, allow family members to draw pictures of flowers at different stages of growth. Pictures of flower growth taken from an encyclopedia will also work for this lesson.

Monday

*My help comes from the LORD,
who made heaven and earth. (Psalm 121)*

Scripture Reading
Psalm 121. After the reading you might begin by saying, "From time to time in life, we need to change our minds about something. Or we may need to change our way of doing something. If we find out that something we thought or something we did was wrong, we need to change.

"Sometimes, though, our thoughts and actions are so deep in us that it is difficult for us to change. We may even believe that we cannot change." Ask, "Have you ever said, 'I couldn't help it?' If you have, you were saying you cannot change."

Share the flowers, bulbs, buds, or pictures. Continue by saying, "These flowers spend their whole lives changing. They start as bulbs, become stems, eventually bloom, and then they start the whole process over again. If God can change the flowers, God can change us." Read the Psalm again. What change is the Psalmist talking about? (change from being in trouble or danger to being safe) Who will bring about this change? (God will save and protect.)

Closing Prayer
Join hands and invite family members to pray in their own words. Ask God to change us where we need changing.

Family Journal

_____
_____
_____
_____
_____
_____
_____

Tuesday

*Now the LORD said to Abram, Go . . .
to the land that I will show you. (Genesis 12:1)*

Scripture Reading

Genesis 12:1-4a. Look at the flowers again. Study their fine details. Allow children an opportunity to ask questions or make observations. Move from this activity to the Bible study by saying something like, "God can certainly do a lot with just a little bit."

Read the passage from Genesis. Ask, "What changes did God make in Abram's life?" (Where he lived, but ultimately his destiny.)

For children, the idea of leaving home is probably frightening. Deal gently with the idea that one day they will grow up, find meaningful work, and perhaps marry and have children. All of these things will be blessings from God and changes in life. This is how we grow and how God guides us into new and important areas of service.

Closing Prayer

Close your worship time in prayer. Ask God to help us not to be afraid of the changes that will come in life. Ask God to work through our changes to help us grow and become stronger and wiser.

Family Journal

_____
_____
_____
_____
_____
_____
_____

Wednesday

*Abraham believed God,
and it was reckoned to him as righteousness.
(Romans 4:3)*

Scripture Reading

Romans 4:1-5. After the reading you might say, "Paul wanted us to notice something very important about the changes in Abraham's life we looked at yesterday. Abraham didn't know how these changes would turn out. He was making changes without any guarantees. Paul called that kind of attitude faith. Abraham had faith in God. He believed in what God was doing and was therefore willing to change and follow a new direction without worrying about the outcome.

"Paul suggested that all of the important changes in life are by faith. Do you agree that is true? Isn't change scary at times? But if we trust God and try to follow God's teachings, the changes that come will be for our benefit. God will take care of the future."

Look at the flowers again. Say, "These don't look very special at the beginning, but at the end they are beautiful! The same will be true for our lives as God changes us and makes us new."

Closing Prayer
Close with a time of prayer. Thank God for loving us and taking care of us.

Family Journal
_____
_____
_____
_____.
_____
_____

Thursday

You must be born from above. (John 3:7)

Scripture Reading
John 3:1-17. After the reading begin by saying something like, "Nicodemus was a teacher of the law of God. He was supposed to know how to help others find their way through life. But when Jesus told Nicodemus that the only way to have a relationship with God was for God to make a birth from above, Nicodemus was shocked.

"'How is that possible?' he wanted to know. Then it was Jesus' turn to be surprised. 'You're a teacher of the Law, and you don't know this?'

"Nicodemus did not believe that God could change him. In fact, he probably was opposed to any kind of change. He was willing to let his life run its course. But if anything new is to happen, if we are to grow and become all that we should be, we must believe that God can change things."

Closing Prayer
Close your worship time in prayer. Ask God to help us not be afraid of change in our lives. Also pray that God will be the one who changes us in other words, from above!

Family Journal

_____

_____

_____

_____

_____

_____

_____

Putting Faith into Action!

Spend some time planting flowers and plants as a family. Call it your Nicodemus garden, or your Abraham garden. Let the growing plants and flowers be a daily reminder of God's power to make all things new.

Fourth Week of Lent
Theme: The Ingredients of Worship

Scripture Readings for the Week
Psalm 95; Exodus 17:1-7; Romans 5:1-11; John 4:5-42

Materials Needed
You will need to supply a pitcher of water and cup of dirt.

Monday *March 11*

> *O come, let us sing to the LORD . . .*
> *Let us come into his presence with thanksgiving.*
> (Psalm 95:6)

Scripture Reading
Psalm 95. Before the reading, say something like, "I could really use a cup of coffee. I'm going to make some. Pour the cup of dirt into the pitcher of water. Stir well. Your children should be screaming at this point.

"I'm making coffee, OK? Does it matter that I used dirt instead of coffee? I mean, as long as I call it coffee, it will be coffee, won't it? You mean I have to use coffee to make coffee? So the ingredients are important!"

This week we are going to look at the ingredients needed for worship. Just because we call something worship does not make it worship. We only worship God when the right parts are present.

Now read the psalm. The first ingredient in true worship is thanksgiving. What does the Psalmist express thanks for? Read the psalm again if needed. Allow everyone an opportunity to identify elements of praise and thanksgiving in the psalm.

Closing Prayer
Close your worship time with prayer. Encourage family members to use their own words to express thanksgiving.

Family Journal
_____
_____
_____
_____
_____
_____
_____

Tuesday

Is the LORD among us or not? (Exodus 17:7)

Scripture Reading

Exodus 17:1-7. Read the brief narrative in Exodus. Ask, "Are these people worshiping God? (No) What ingredient was missing for them?" (They did not believe that God was with them or for them.)

Continue by saying, "When we worship it is important to remember that God is always with us. If we are thinking about what we are going to do later, or if we are angry with someone, we are not thinking about God. We behave like God is not there."

Why did the people of Israel believe that God was not there? (because they had no water) Ask, "What sort of things might cause us to think God is not with us?" Allow everyone to come up with their own answers. Say, "When we worship, our first and last thought should be on the presence of God."

Closing Prayer

Lead your family in prayer. Ask God to help us to be aware of God's constant presence in our world and in our lives.

Family Journal

_____
_____
_____
_____
_____
_____

Wednesday

But God proved his love for us in that while we still were sinners Christ died for us. (Romans 5:8)

Scripture Reading

Romans 5: 1-11. After the reading, you might say something like, "The people of Israel doubted God's care for them because they were without water. Paul, though, said that suffering creates an opportunity for us to learn endurance, that is, to hang in there and not be quitters.

"One of the important ingredients, then, that we bring to worship is our real selves. We are weak, but God loves us anyway. We are sinners, but God still loves us. Even before we tried to worship, God loved us. Even though we don't even know how to worship the way we should, God still wants us to try. We don't have to pretend to be something we are not. God wants the real 'us' there."

Closing Prayer

Join hands and invite family members to close in prayer. Thank God for allowing us to come and worship just like we are.

Family Journal

_____

_____

_____

_____

_____

_____

Thursday

God is spirit, and those who worship [God] must worship in spirit and truth. (John 4:24)

Scripture Reading

John 4:5-42. The final two ingredients of worship are named in this story. Read the story and see if family members can pick out the two ingredients. They are spirit and truth.

To worship in spirit means to worship with our whole selves. Worship is not just a mental thing, nor is it purely an emotional thing. It is a whole person thing. We worship God with our minds, our hearts, and our bodies.

To worship in truth means that we tell God the truth about ourselves. The woman Jesus talked to wanted to slide easily past the truth.

Only as we tell God the truth about our lives our failures, our fears, and our behavior can we expect to really worship.

Closing Prayer

Close your worship time in prayer. Ask God to help us understand how we might mix all the ingredients of worship together in our lives and really know that God is with us.

Family Journal

_____

_____

_____

_____

_____

Putting Faith into Action!

Attend a worship service. It might be a Sunday service or a special community service. Before going, review the ingredients of worship. If a printed program is available, use it to guide children through the different areas of worship offered in the service. Encourage family members to watch for opportunities to express thanks. Remind everyone that we must be honest about who we are and seek to worship God with our whole lives.

Fifth Week of Lent
Theme: Learning to See God

Scripture Readings for the Week
Psalm 23; 1 Samuel 16:1-13; Ephesians 5:8-14; John 9:1-41

Materials Needed
Make an eye chart like those found in an optometrist's office. Start off with a big E. Follow with a line of smaller letters in random order. Let the last three lines spell out "God is Love." The object is reinforce the idea of learning to see God in less than obvious ways.

Monday

Surely goodness and mercy shall follow me . . .
(Psalm 23:6)

Scripture Reading
Psalm 23. This well known psalm is often used at funerals. It offers a comforting message. But the psalm itself is really about helping us to be aware of God's careful attention to God's people.

Give everyone an eye exam. Help little ones discover God in the eye chart. After everyone passes the exam, read the psalm for today.

Encourage family members to listen carefully for all the ways the Psalmist was able to see God in the world.

Using examples from the psalm, call on volunteers to name some ways we might see God in our world.

Closing Prayer
Close your worship time together. Thank God for being everywhere in our world and in our lives.

Family Journal
_____
_____
_____
_____
_____

Tuesday

. . . But the LORD looks on the heart. (1 Sam 16:7c)

Scripture Reading
1 Samuel 16:1-13. Before the reading, say something like, "One of the ways we learn to see

God in our world is by learning to see the world the way God sees it. The story in our Scripture Reading today is an example of the way God sees the world." Read the story of the anointing of David as king of Israel.

After the reading, ask family members what they noticed in the story. What sort of man was Samuel looking for? Why wasn't the obvious choice the best choice? (because it wasn't the one God wanted)

What do we learn about God's view of the world when we notice that David was the weakest and least likely choice? (that God often chooses to work through weakness rather than strength) If God chooses to work through weakness, where might we find God in our world? (in the midst of the weak and powerless people of our world)

Closing Prayer
Close your time of worship in a few moments of silence. Ask God to help us learn to see the world the way God sees the world, especially the people of the world.

Family Journal

_____
_____
_____
_____
_____
_____

Wednesday

Try to find out what is pleasing to the Lord.
(Ephesians 5:10)

Scripture Reading
Ephesians 5:8-14. After the reading, show everyone the eye chart again. Have family members look at the chart with one eye closed. Can they still see it? Yes. Then have family members look at the chart with both eyes closed. Can they still see the chart? No.

"In this scripture, Paul told his friends that they must wake from sleep. In other words, they must open their eyes in order to see what God is doing. What do you think he means?" Allow time for discussion.

Continue by saying, "When Paul said we must wake up, he was telling us something very important. If we are not careful, we will get lazy or tired. Following God and trying to see God in the world is hard work. If we fall asleep or stop paying attention, we might miss our opportunity to see God.

"Paul wanted us to live our lives awake! In other words, we are to keep our eyes open and pay close attention. If we watch carefully, we will learn to see God in many different ways."

Closing Prayer

Close your worship time in prayer. Thank God for the gift of rest. Ask God, however, to help us go through life with our eyes open.

Family Journal

_____
_____
_____
_____
_____
_____

Thursday

Jesus said to him, You have seen him . . . (John 9:37)

Scripture Reading

John 9:1-41. This is a long reading. In order to hold the attention of children (and probably adults as well!), the story should be read in a lively manner. This is a three-act drama read it as such. If you are comfortable with the story, tell it rather than read it. The focal verses for our purposes are 35-41.

After the reading, ask, "Why do you think the Jewish leaders were unwilling to see God at work in Jesus?" Allow time for discussion. "If the Jewish leaders had admitted that Jesus was sent from God, it would have undermined their power and authority. The lesson we learn here is this: In order to see God, we must be willing to let God do what God wants to do even to let God surprise us."

Pull out the eye chart once again. Hold it up where the letters and words are facing away from you. Say something like, "I know what this chart says. It says God is angry. Right?" (Of course, it does not. It says God is Love.) Get into an argument with family members about what the chart says, but refuse to look at it. Say, "I don't have to look at it I know what it says!"

This was the exact attitude of the Jewish leaders in our reading today. Read the closing verses again (9:35-41). Continue by saying, "Because they claimed to 'see' God, and refused to look at anything else, they were really blind to God's presence in our world."

Closing Prayer

Close your worship time in prayer. Ask God to help us learn to see the world the way God sees it, and in the process, learn to see God in the world.

Family Journal

_____

_____

_____

_____

_____

_____

Putting Faith into Action!

Take a nature walk as a family. As you walk along, try to notice all the ways God is present in the world of nature. If we can learn to see God in the world of plants and birds, we should also be able to see God in the world of people. Spend some time with people this week. Look for God in them. Let them see God in you.

Sixth Week of Lent[2]
Theme: Jesus, the Humble King

Scripture Readings for the Week
Psalm 118:1-2, 19-20; Isaiah 50:4-9a; Philippians 2:5-11; Matthew 21:1-11

Materials Needed
Gather some green leafy branches. Palm leaves would be ideal if available.

Monday

Open to me the gates of righteousness, that I may enter through them and give thanks to the LORD. (Psalm 118:19)

Scripture Reading
Psalm 118:1-2, 19-20. After the reading, distribute a palm branch to every family member. Say something like, "In the ancient world, kings were greeted with the waving of banners and branches much like these. It was one way people had of showing honor and respect.

"The Psalmist is picturing a scene like this. Instead of praising an earthly king, however, it is God who is praised in these verses. Praise and thanksgiving are the correct responses we make to God. As we move closer to Easter, let us fill our hearts with gratitude for all that God has done."

Closing Prayer
Close with prayers of thanksgiving and praise. Guide children by your example, but let them come up with their own prayers.

Family Journal
_____
_____
_____
_____
_____

Tuesday

It is the LORD GOD who helps me. (Isaiah 50:9)

Scripture Reading
Read the words from Isaiah 50. These words describe in graphic detail exactly how Jesus was treated by leaders in Jerusalem. One day people were cheering him and welcoming him to Jerusalem. A few days later they were beating

him and pulling out his beard. Jesus knew this. Even as he entered the city, he knew.

Ask, "Why didn't Jesus run away? Why didn't he fight for his life? If he was a king, why didn't he call for an army to help him?" Allow family members time to discuss this for awhile.

Continue by saying, "Jesus entered Jerusalem as king, but as a humble king. Jesus was not a warrior; he was the Savior. He did not come to take life; Jesus came to give life. For that reason he suffered all the things Isaiah saw centuries before."

Closing Prayer

Close with a few moments of silence. Thank God for sending us a humble king, and open us to Jesus' entry in our lives each day.

Family Journal

_____

_____

_____

_____

_____

_____

_____

Wednesday

Let this mind be in you
that was in Christ Jesus . . . (Philippians 2:5)

Scripture Reading

Philippians 2:5-11. After the reading, say something like, "Many people believe that these verses are a very old Easter hymn, perhaps even one of the first ever written. The song traces the whole life of Jesus.

"The most important part of the song focuses on the humility or lowliness of Jesus. Jesus became a servant, a lowly working person, and died on a cross. He humbled himself in death for us.

"The celebration of Easter is all about the death and resurrection of Jesus, but today we notice the humility of Jesus. Jesus did not try to force people to do things. He asked them and led them as a humble servant.

"As we wave our palm leaves and shout 'Hooray for the king,' remember the kind of king he was."

Closing Prayer

Join hands and invite family members to pray in their own words. Thank God for taking away our sin and offering forgiveness to us through Jesus.

Family Journal

_____
_____
_____
_____
_____
_____

Thursday

*Look, your king is coming to you,
humble, and mounted on a donkey. (Matt 21:5)*

Scripture Reading

Matthew 21:1-11. Read these verses carefully. Describe the scene. Ask family members, "Why were these people so happy? Why were they so glad that Jesus had come to Jerusalem?" Allow time for discussion.

The crowd hailed Jesus as king, but not as a humble king. They wanted a son of David. This means they wanted Jesus to be a great warrior in the same way King David was, but Jesus was not a warrior king. Jesus arrived in Jerusalem, riding a donkey, not the white horse of a conquering hero. Later, when the people realized the kind of king he was, they threw their palm branches away and lost interest in Jesus.

Ask, "Why did Jesus choose to be a humble king rather than a warrior king?" Allow time for discussion. "Warriors kill people. Jesus came to save people."

Closing Prayer

Close your worship time in prayer. Ask God to help us follow the humble king and be humble ourselves. Then, write in the Family Journal ways that our lives can show more humility.

Family Journal

_____
_____
_____
_____
_____
_____

Putting Faith into Action!

A humble king serves others. Since Jesus wants us to follow his example, we should be humble servants as well. Look for ways to serve each other today. Share chores with other family members. Do special acts of kindness for everyone. If time permits, seek to extend the role of servant beyond your family. Rake your neighbor's yard or cut the grass. Take a friend or family out to lunch, or invite them over for a meal.

Holy Week

Whoever serves me must follow me, and where I am, there will my servant be also. (John 12:26)

Many churches observe Holy Week services. If a church in your area observes Holy Week, your family might profit from attending these daily services. These services can be augmented with the following activities.

Although the central symbol of Holy Week is the Cross, other objects also serve to move us through this dramatic moment in the life of our Lord. Items needed for this week include perfume (Monday), two paper clips (Tuesday), a piece of bread (Wednesday), a bowl of water and a wash cloth (Thursday), a wooden cross (Friday), and a roll of masking tape (Saturday). Also plan to attend a Maundy Thursday service.

This week calls for more effort in preparation. For Christians, however, this should be the single most important week of the whole year.

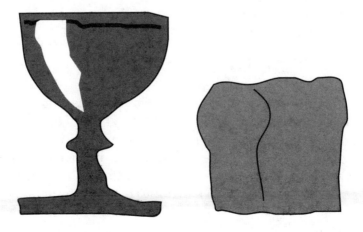

Holy Week[3]
Theme: The Last Week of Jesus' Life

Monday

Mary took a pound of costly perfume . . .
anointed Jesus' feet and wiped them with her hair.
(John 12:3)

Scripture Reading

John 12:1-11. After the reading, open a bottle of perfume or cologne. It will not take long for the fragrance to fill the room. Pass the bottle around; allow everyone a chance to smell the fragrance.

Say something like, "Mary was overcome with feelings of gratitude, love, and sorrow. Jesus was very important to her and her family. She knew he was about to face his death. She wanted to do something that would show how much she cared for him.

"The perfume she poured on his feet was very expensive. If we used money from today to buy the perfume, it would cost as much as a car. But Mary was not concerned with the cost. She was only concerned with showing Jesus her love."

Closing Prayer

As we move toward Resurrection Day, let us also be willing to find ways to show Jesus our love for him. Pray, and ask God to help us as we try to serve and follow our Lord.

Family Journal

_____
_____
_____
_____
_____
_____

Tuesday

Whoever serves me must follow me . . . (John 12:26)

Scripture Reading

John 12:20-36. This is a difficult reading, especially for children. The point is simple, however. In order for Jesus to complete his work, he had to change through death. In order for us to follow Jesus and complete his work, we must change through obedience.

Show everyone the two paper clips. Take one and bend it out of shape. Say something like, "This paper clip is just a piece of wire bent into a certain shape. As a straight piece of wire it is not able to be used as a paper clip. Only when the wire is bent into the proper shape can it be used to hold papers. That is what Jesus is saying to us. Only as we allow Jesus to form us into the right shape will we be able to help others. Jesus himself was also shaped by death to be our servant king."

Closing Prayer

Close this day in prayer. Ask God to help us bend into the right shape. Be sure to express thanksgiving for God's presence in our lives.

Family Journal

_____
_____
_____
_____
_____
_____
_____

Wednesday

Very truly, I tell you, one of you will betray me.
(John 13:21)

Scripture Reading

John 13:21-32. After the reading, show everyone the piece of bread. Say something like, "In Jesus' time, the highest compliment you could pay someone was to share bread with them. Sharing bread with others was like telling them you loved them. It was a way of demonstrating friendship. Jesus was betrayed by Judas after they shared bread.

"We must be careful not to betray Jesus. He loves us and we are close to him. If we decide we want something more than we want him, however, we end trading Jesus for what we want instead. It is the same as Judas sharing bread with Jesus, then turning him over to the police."

Closing Prayer

Jesus wants us to share bread with him and love him. Let us pray and ask God to help us never betray our friendship with Jesus.

Family Journal

_____
_____
_____
_____
_____
_____

Holy Thursday:
Maundy Thursday

*Very truly, I tell you, servants
are not greater than their master . . . (John 13:16)*

Scripture Reading

John 13:1-17; 31b-35. (The word "maundy" comes from the Latin word *maundus*, which means to command. The word refers to the institution of the Lord's Supper. As you will notice, however, the Lord's Supper is not mentioned in the Gospel of John. Instead we have Jesus washing the feet of his disciples. The act of footwashing can be a powerful illustration of servanthood. If, however, you are uncomfortable with the idea, simply adapt this lesson to a celebration of the Lord's Supper in your own home. Another option would be to attend a Maundy Thursday service at a local church.)

Carefully read the story of Jesus' act of washing the feet of his disciples. You might say something like, "Jesus wanted to drive home the point that his primary role in this world was that of a servant. Simon Peter resisted this act of humiliation until Jesus explained that it was the only way to have a real relationship with him. At that, Peter was ready for a bath!"

Introduce the basin and towel. Continue by saying, "Let us demonstrate our love for each other and our willingness to follow Jesus as servants by washing each other's feet." (This has the potential to be giggly for children. Why not let it be a fun time? The point is made whether we laugh at it or not.)

Closing Prayer

Close your worship time in prayer. Thank God for including us in God's family.

Family Journal

_____

_____

_____

_____

_____

_____

_____

Good Friday

It is finished. (John 19:30)

Scripture Reading

John 18:1 19:42. Throughout this book, the Friday activities have all been "Putting Faith into Action." That theme may continue today. Introduce the wooden cross you have made. Continue by saying, "Good Friday is the day we remember the death of Jesus. Why would we call such a terrible day good?" Allow family members to discuss.

"Good Friday is called good because of the good that comes from the cross. Because of Jesus' death and resurrection, we have life eternal. Good Friday is an opportunity for us to think deeply about the price of God's love. Holding this cross in our hands helps us to understand how far God was willing to go to save us and help us."

Pass the cross to each family member. Encourage members to discuss how they feel as they look at the cross.

Closing Prayer

Allow everyone an opportunity to pray. Thank God for what Jesus did on the cross for us.

Family Journal

_____
_____
_____
_____
_____
_____
_____

Holy Saturday

Make it as secure as you can. (Matt 27:65)

Scripture Reading

Matthew 27:57-66. After the reading, take a strip of masking tape and tape everyone's hands together. Not too tight! Continue by saying, "Pilate told his soldiers to make the tomb as secure as they could. The authority and power of the Roman empire was positioned to keep Jesus in the tomb.

"But the power of Rome was no match for the power of God. Tell everyone to tear their hands free from the tape. It was easier for God to raise Jesus from the dead than it was for you to tear the tape from your hands. The gift of the resurrection reveals God's desire to defeat death in our lives and in our world."

Closing Prayer

Close your worship time. Thank God for unsealing the tomb sealed by Pilate's order. Pray with the Psalmist: "I believe that I shall see the goodness of the Lord in the land of the living. Wait for the Lord; be strong, and let your heart take courage; wait for the Lord!" (Psalm 27:13-14)

Family Journal

_____

_____

_____

_____

_____

_____

Easter Sunday

So if you have been raised with Christ, seek the things that are above, where Christ is, seated at the right hand of God.
Colossians 3:1

Christmas and Easter are such important days in the Christian year that we ought to devote special attention to their observance.

Easter Sunday
Theme: When the Lord Calls Your Name

I have seen the Lord (John 20:18b)

Scripture Readings

Psalm 118:1-2, 14-24; Acts 10:34-43; Colossians 3:1-4; John 20:1-18. Focus on the verses from John 20:1-18. (Hopefully, this will be a day filled with exciting observances. You may attend a sunrise service. The afternoon may be filled with family activities and a big meal.)

Read the verses carefully, with dramatic flair. Encourage family members to listen for the moment when someone in the story finally believes that Jesus is alive. It is not the empty tomb. It is not the grave clothes. Only when Jesus calls Mary by name does she believe that he is alive. Continue by saying, "The Resurrection is not simply something we believe in. It is something we live in. God calls each of us, by name, to follow Jesus and love him. That is possible because Jesus is alive."

Closing Prayer

Close your worship time in a few moments of silence. Thank God for the promise of new life and life eternal that comes to us through the Resurrection.

Family Journal

_____
_____
_____
_____
_____
_____
_____

First Week after Easter
Theme: Flesh and Bone Savior

Scripture Readings for the Week
Psalm 16; Acts 2:14a, 22-32; 1 Peter 1:3-9; John 20:19-31

Materials Needed
Use your own hand to demonstrate the importance of God incarnate a flesh and bone savior.

Monday

The LORD is my right hand. (Psalm 16:8)

Scripture Reading
Psalm 16. Be sure to emphasize verse 16:8 "The Lord is at my right hand." After the reading, you might begin by saying, "Obviously, God is different from us. We are flesh and bone (show everyone your hand); God is spirit. We live and die; God lives forever. We know very little; God knows everything.

"But even though we are different from God, faithful people throughout history have talked about God as if God were right in the room with them. The Psalmist does that in our reading today. God called it a 'refuge.' A refuge is a safe hiding place. The Psalmist also says that God is at his right hand (show your hand again).

"How is it possible to believe that a God who is so different from us can still be very near to us?" Allow family members a few moments to offer suggestions.

Closing Prayer
Continue by saying, "This week we will learn how Jesus made it easier for us to feel God's closeness. But for now, let's pray and ask God to be near to us as close as our right hand."

Family Journal
_____
_____
_____
_____
_____
_____
_____

Tuesday

This Jesus God raised up,
and of that all of us are witnesses. (Acts 2:32)

Scripture Reading

Acts 2:14a, 22-35. Encourage family members to listen for the word hand or hands or handed as you read the text for today. After the reading, you might say something like, "Peter preached this sermon to the people who witnessed the death of Jesus. They saw him bleed and die. They knew he was a real flesh-and-bone human being.

"But he was more than just another man. He was the Messiah. Because Jesus was the Messiah, God exalted (promoted, elevated, lifted up) him to a place of great honor. Jesus sits at God's right hand!

"Why is that important for us?" Allow family members to think about this question for awhile. Encourage creative thinking. Continue by saying, "Jesus, a flesh-and-bone messiah, sits at God's right hand. The significance is that all people all flesh-and-bone people now have a way to approach God. God who is different and invisible is now approachable through Jesus, the flesh-and-bone messiah."

Closing Prayer

Encourage family members to think about the discussion today. After a few moments of silence, close in prayer. Thank God for creating a way for us to approach God.

Family Journal

_____
_____
_____
_____
_____
_____
_____

Wednesday

Although you have not seen him, you love him.
(1 Peter 1:8)

Scripture Reading

1 Peter 1:3-9. After the reading, you might say something like, "The writer of this letter addresses a special group of people (review v. 8). These people came after the life and death of Jesus. They had only heard about him; they never saw him or heard him first hand. Also, they would have to continue in faith without seeing him. We are in exactly the same situation.

"Even though we believe we have a flesh-and-bone savior (use your hand to illustrate) who sits at the right hand of God, we can't see him. We came after his life and death. Jesus is as invisible to us as God is. So how does a flesh-and-bone savior help us?" Allow family members to struggle with this question for a while.

Continue by saying, "There is at least one benefit to believing in a flesh-and-bone savior. Because Jesus was fully human, we can be sure that he fully understands our suffering, pain, and disappointment (read v. 6).

"We do not worship a God who is distant and unconcerned about our needs as humans. We worship and serve a God who loves us enough to become one of us."

Closing Prayer
Hold hands as you close your worship time in prayerful silence. Encourage family members to feel the warm hand of the person next to them. The human hand is a reminder of God's closeness. Offer thanks to God for being so near to us.

Family Journal
_____
_____
_____
_____
_____
_____
_____

Thursday

Do not doubt but believe. (John 20:27)

Scripture Reading
John 20:19-31. Read or tell this story with some feeling. Help family members feel the drama. After the story, you might say something like, "Thomas found it hard to believe Jesus was alive. He had seen Jesus die on a cross. Even though his friends assured him it was true, Thomas wondered how Jesus could be alive. Thomas was determined not to be fooled. He announced that he would not believe until he saw Jesus' hands and the wound in Jesus' side.

"Jesus appeared to Thomas and allowed him to see his hands and wounded side. This experience moved Thomas to make an important statement. He bowed before Jesus and said, 'My Lord and my God.' Thomas understood that God had become fully known through the flesh and bone of Jesus.

"Jesus also made an important statement important for us. He praised Thomas for recognizing God's presence in Jesus' flesh, but he went on to praise even higher those who reach the same conclusion without ever seeing Jesus' hands or feet. That includes all of us. We weren't there to see Jesus die or raised from the dead, and yet we believe. Jesus told Thomas that our belief is special."

Closing Prayer

Close your worship time in prayer. Thank God for becoming fully known in Jesus' flesh and bone.

Family Journal

_____
_____
_____
_____
_____
_____
_____

Putting Faith into Action!

God continues to become real in our world through the flesh and bone of faithful servants people like us. That means we are able to help make God known to others by the things we do with our hands and feet.

Therefore, do something with your hands and feet today that make God known. Visit a sick person, provide assistance to a person in need, clean someone's house, or bake someone a cake. As you do, remember, God is at your right hand, and Jesus is at God's right hand!

Second Week after Easter
Theme: In the Breaking of Bread

Scripture Readings for the Week
Psalm 116:1-4, 12-19; Acts 2:14a, 36-41; 1 Peter 1:17-23; Luke 24:13-35

Materials Needed
Use a loaf of bread as a worship tool this week.

Monday

What shall I return to the LORD for all his bounty to me?
(Psalm 116:12)

Scripture Reading
Psalm 116:1-4, 12-19. Emphasize 116:12. After the reading, give everyone a slice of bread. You might say something like, "Some people in our world have only this much food for a whole day. We eat more than this at one meal. This is what the Psalmist meant by the word 'bounty.' God shows love and compassion for us by providing richly for our needs. But we must ask with Psalmist, 'What shall I return to the Lord for all this bounty?'

"If we learn to see God in the blessings of life, it will teach us gratitude. Let's give thanks right now for all the ways God takes care of us."

Closing Prayer
Encourage everyone to offer their own prayer of thanksgiving for God's blessings. Be sure to express thanksgiving for God's presence in our lives.

Family Journal
_____
_____
_____
_____
_____
_____

Tuesday

They devoted themselves to the apostles' teaching and fellowship, to the breaking of bread and the prayers.
(Acts 2:42)

Scripture Reading
Acts 2:14a, 36-42. Emphasize 2:42 as you read these verses. After the reading, you might ask, "What does it mean that all these Christians

devoted themselves to the 'breaking of bread.' Allow time for responses.

Continue by saying, "The expression 'breaking bread' had two meanings in the early church. Breaking bread together meant sharing a meal together. This was even understood and practiced among non-Christians.

"The other meaning, however, was uniquely Christian. Breaking bread together was a way of celebrating God's presence in Jesus. The broken bread was seen as a symbol of Jesus' broken body. The sharing of this special bread brought the people together in a powerful way. They were united, joined to each other by the sharing of bread."

Pass around a single slice of bread. Tell everyone to break off a small piece. You might say something like, "Because God has provided this bread for our health, and because God gave Jesus to us for our salvation, we share life together even as we share this bread together."

Closing Prayer

Give thanks to God for the bread and for the Bread of Life. Allow everyone an opportunity to offer a prayer of thanksgiving.

Family Journal

_____
_____
_____
_____
_____
_____

Wednesday

Love one another deeply from the heart. (1 Peter 1:22)

Scripture Reading

1 Peter 1:17-23. Although the writer of 1 Peter does not mention bread in these verses, he emphasizes the unique bond that exists for followers of Christ. After the reading, pass a piece of bread to each family member. Tell members to break off a piece for themselves. When the bread gets back to you, break your piece into two pieces.

Continue by saying, "The bread symbolizes that we are together as a family. God provides for us, and God saves us through Jesus. We are also part of a wider family. Other Christians share the bread (show the extra piece). We are united to these people because of the blessings of God." Read 1:22 again.

Closing Prayer

Close your worship time in prayer. Ask God to help us love one another.

Family Journal

_____
_____
_____
_____
_____
_____

Thursday

He had been made known to them
in the breaking of the break. (Luke 24:35)

Scripture Reading

Luke 24:13-35. Before reading these verses, you might say, "This is an important and powerful story. It reveals the struggle the church has always had with the Resurrection. Even the witnesses at the empty tomb did not know what to make of it. Only after Jesus appeared to them was there understanding and acceptance.

"But what of the rest of us? How are we supposed to experience the resurrection for ourselves? Is it enough to simply enjoy the experiences of others? Is it enough to simply take on faith that the tomb was empty? The story we are about to hear suggests another way." Read the passage from Luke.

After the reading, introduce another piece of bread. Continue by saying, "Luke's story suggests that the resurrected Jesus continues to be available to us as we break bread together not just at meal times, but especially as we celebrate the Lord's Supper. As we share the bread, we have an opportunity to recognize Jesus, to see him, to enjoy his presence."

Share the bread as before. As the bread is passed, you might say, "We welcome you, O Lord, to our sharing of bread together."

Closing Prayer

Finish your family worship with prayer. Thank God for life and richness of life with others.

Family Journal

_____
_____
_____
_____
_____
_____

Putting Faith into Action!

Hold your own Lord's Supper in your home. Bake bread, and put grape juice in special glasses. As you share the bread and juice, be sure to acknowledge the presence of Christ in the midst of your family worship. Turn the whole service into a rich, family event.

Third Week after Easter
Theme: Hearing the Right Call

Scripture Readings for the Week
Psalm 23; Acts 2:42-47; 1 Peter 2:19-25; John 10:1-10

Materials Needed
Provide construction paper and markers. Encourage everyone to make a colorful name tag for themselves. Provide tape or safety pins to attach the name tags. Be sure to wear them during every worship time you have this week.

Monday

The LORD is my shepherd, I shall not want. (Psalm 23:1)

Scripture Reading
Psalm 23. We have already looked at this psalm in connection with learning how to see God. We consider it again in the context of identity. In other words, we know who we are when we know whose we are.

Have some fun making the name tags. Spend some time talking about how names were selected or what names might mean. If anyone is named in honor of some family member, talk about how that came about. Say something like, "Most people like to be called by their own name. It is part of who we are as persons part of our identity."

After reading the psalm, continue by saying, "The writer of this psalm must have known a great deal about sheep. He knew that sheep need a shepherd. That's who sheep are animals that need someone to take care of them. The writer of the psalm was not afraid to compare himself to a sheep. 'The Lord is my shepherd.'

"This is a good thing to understand. We are known by who we follow. If we follow outlaws, we are known as outlaws. If we follow a shepherd we are known as sheep. In this case, we are known as the sheep of a caring and loving God. That is not a bad way to be known."

Closing Prayer
Close in prayer. Thank God for knowing us by name, but also for knowing us by need.

Family Journal

_____

_____

_____

_____

_____

_____

_____

Tuesday

*They spent much time together . . . praising God
and having the good will of all the people. (Acts 2:46-47)*

Scripture Reading

Acts 2:42-47. Make sure everyone has their name tag. After reading the verses from Acts, you might say, "These verses paint a picture of people who really cared about each other. If we were going to come up with a name for these people, something to call them, what would it be?" Read the verses again. Point out the generous sharing, faithful devotion, and general goodwill created by these people. Let family members suggest names from these descriptions. For example, they might have been called the food-sharing-people.

After a few moments you might say, "Of course we don't have to come up with a name for these people. They already have a name. These are followers of Christ; they are

Christians. That is their name, and that is what they do they follow Christ."

Closing Prayer

Close in prayer. Thank God for our names. Ask God to help us live out our lives known by a new name: followers of Christ.

Family Journal

_____

_____

_____

_____

_____

_____

_____

Wednesday

For to this you have been called. (1 Peter 2:21)

Scripture Reading

1 Peter 2:19-25. Make sure everyone is wearing their name tag. You might begin by saying, "Your first and last name identifies you as being part of this family. People know whose family you belong to because of your name."

After reading the scripture passage for today, continue by saying, "Yesterday we learned that Christians are people who share together and seek to love one another. In our reading today we learn something else about who we are. Following Jesus means letting Jesus be our example. We learn from him how to live our lives.

"The writer of 1 Peter said that since Jesus did not fight back when he was beaten, we should also avoid fighting back. When we refuse to return anger for anger, we show everyone our true identity. We show people we are Christians, followers and imitators of Jesus."

Closing Prayer

Allow everyone an opportunity to pray. Ask God to help us follow Jesus' example.

Family Journal

_____

_____

_____

_____

_____

_____

_____

Thursday

I am the good shepherd. (John 10:11)

Scripture Reading

John 10:1-10. Make new name tags for everyone. This time, in addition to their name, add the words, "Follower of Jesus," "the Good Shepherd." Make sure everyone is wearing their name tags before you begin.

After the reading, you might say something like, "Jesus calls himself the Good Shepherd. He was probably thinking about Psalm 23. He wants us to follow him. He also says we should know the sound of his voice. What do you think he means by that?" Allow a few moments to think about what knowing Jesus' voice might mean.

Continue by saying, "Knowing Jesus' voice means knowing what he would have us to do. If someone tells us to be selfish and uncaring about other people, we know that is not the voice of Jesus. If someone wants us to hurt someone, we know that is not the voice of Jesus. Knowing the voice of Jesus means knowing what Jesus would and would not say.

"We are Jesus' sheep. We follow where he leads. That is part of our name of who we are."

Closing Prayer

Join hands and invite family members to offer a prayer in their own words. Thank God for giving us a new name.

Family Journal

_____

_____

_____

_____

_____

_____

_____

Putting Faith into Action!

Call someone you haven't heard from lately. Tell that person what you've been learning and that you just wanted to hear his/her voice.

Fourth Week after Easter
Theme: God's House

Scripture Readings for the Week
Psalm 31:1-5, 15-16; Acts 7:55-60; 1 Peter 2:2-10; John 14:1-14

Materials Needed
Provide drawing paper and colored pencils. Encourage family members to draw a picture of what they think the perfect house would look like. After the pictures are finished, allow everyone an opportunity to explain their drawing.

Monday

In you, O LORD, I seek refuge. (Psalm 31:1)

Scripture Reading
Psalm 31:1-5, 15-16. After the reading you might ask, "What are some of the things a house can do for us?" (keep us warm in winter and dry during rains, keep us safe during danger) Continue by saying, "Another word for a safe place is the word 'refuge.' The Psalmist talks about taking refuge in God's presence.

"As we look about our home, we feel safe and protected here. As we live and serve God, we find that God is also a safe place, a refuge, a home."

Closing Prayer
Close your worship time in prayer. Thank God for caring for us and providing a safe home for us.

Family Journal

_____

_____

_____

_____

_____

_____

_____

Tuesday

Lord Jesus, receive my spirit. (Acts 7:59)

Scripture Reading
Acts 7:55-60. Ask if family members want to make any changes in their houses. After the reading, continue by saying, "The story of Stephen serves to remind us how dangerous

and crazy the world can be. We might even be tempted to ask 'Why didn't God protect Stephen and save him?' That is a tough question. We really cannot know the answer.

"What we can know is how Stephen felt about God as the crowd was killing him. Stephen looked into the heavens and saw Jesus standing at God's right hand. As he died, Stephen prayed, 'Lord, receive my spirit.' Stephen found a refuge or a place of comfort in God, even as he faced an angry mob. Stephen was aware of God's presence even as the crowd set out to kill him.

"Living in the world as God's children does not mean we always get our way. We don't always get what we want. We are not always safe from evil people. The promise we have, however, is that we are always in God's sight. God is always with us. God's presence is a refuge that comforts us when the world goes crazy."

Closing Prayer

Close your worship time in prayer. Thank God for being with us even when things are scary.

Family Journal

_____
_____
_____
_____
_____
_____
_____

Wednesday

*Like living stones, let yourselves
be built into a spiritual house. (1 Peter 2:5)*

Scripture Reading

1 Peter 2:2-10. Emphasize 2:4-5. After the reading, you might say something like, "God is interested in building a house too, not a house made out of wood and bricks, but a spiritual house. A spiritual house is a house built out of love, forgiveness, kindness, and generosity."

Ask, "How will God build this spiritual house using the things we just named? How can that be done?" Allow family members time to answer. After a few moments, continue by saying, "God will build this spiritual house by using our lives, our faith in Christ, our kindness, our love, our forgiveness. We are the building blocks."

Ask again, "Who will live in the house that God builds, using us as building blocks?" Allow family members time to answer. God wants to build a house big enough for everyone to live in and find refuge.

Closing Prayer

Close your worship time in a few moments of silence. Ask God to help us as we try to be good building blocks for God's spiritual house.

Family Journal

_____
_____
_____
_____
_____
_____
_____

Thursday

And if I go and prepare a place for you,
I will come again and take you to myself. (John 14:3)

Scripture Reading

John 14:1-14. Provide paper and colored pencils. Encourage everyone to draw a picture of God's house. (It's okay if it looks like a church the symbol of God's inclusive family.)

After having some fun with the drawings, read the verses from John 14. After the reading, you might say something like, "John says that in God's house there is a room for everyone. Look at the picture of God's house that you drew.

Where are you in the picture?" (If family members did not draw themselves in the picture, have them do so now.)

Closing Prayer

How does Jesus say we get to our room? (by following him and doing what he did) Let's pray together right now to always work to make sure people know that God has room for them. Pray also that we remember that we have a room in God's house.

Family Journal

_____
_____
_____
_____
_____
_____
_____

Putting Faith into Action!

Buy some wood and build a bird house for your yard. Fill it with bird seed. Watch for the day when birds come to visit the house. Let the birds of the air be a constant reminder of God's desire to make a home for all of us.

Fifth Week after Easter
Theme: How To Say, 'I Love You, God'

Scripture Readings for the Week
Psalm 66:8-20; Acts 17:22-31; 1 Peter 3:13-22; John 14:15-21

Materials Needed
You will need a large sheet of paper or poster board and a marker or crayon as your worship tools this week.

Monday

Blessed be God. (Psalm 66:20)

Scripture Reading
Psalm 66:8-20. Before reading the psalm for today, place the poster board in front of everyone. You might say something like, "There are many ways to let people know how much we love them. We may do the obvious thing and simply say, 'I love you,' but there are other ways as well. Use your imagination and think of some ways we let people know we love them." Adults should be ready to get this moving. You might describe how it feels for someone to say please or thank you. Record all responses on the poster board.

After several minutes, read the psalm for today. Continue by saying, "The Psalmist discusses several ways we can say 'I love you' to God. What are some of the suggestions mentioned?" Read the psalm again.

Continue, "It is important to let people know we love them and appreciate them. It is also important for us to love and appreciate God."

Closing Prayer
Encourage family members to express their love for God in prayer.

Family Journal
_____
_____
_____
_____
_____
_____

Tuesday

What therefore you worship as unknown, this I proclaim to you. (Acts 17:23)

Acts 17:22-31. After the reading, you might say something like, "Most people want to know God and love God. We don't always know how to do it, but most of us want to. The story of Paul in Athens is a story about people who wanted to love God so much that they built altars (worship places) to all of the gods they had ever heard of. They even built one to any 'unknown god,' just to make sure they didn't miss any.

"Paul did not scold the people of Athens for having all of these altars. He knew it was their best effort to try and worship God. So instead of criticizing them, he tried to help them. Paul told them he knew who the unknown God was. He told them about creation and beauty and finally about Jesus.

"Not everyone heard what he said. Sometimes we make up our mind about something, and it is hard to change. But a few people believed what he was saying to them.

"Here is the point. Everybody is looking for God, even though some people are looking in the wrong way. If we really love God and love people, rather than criticizing the efforts of others, we will try to find a way to help them."

Closing Prayer

Close in prayer. Ask God to help us love God the way we should and to also help others who are trying to find a God to love.

Family Journal

_____
_____
_____
_____
_____
_____
_____

Wednesday

In your hearts sanctify Christ as Lord. (1 Peter 3:15)

Scripture Reading

1 Peter 3:13-22. Emphasize verses 13-17. After the reading, you might say something like, "When we love God, our lives begin to change in some pretty interesting ways. We start thinking about things differently, and soon we begin to act differently.

"In our world, if someone hurts us or takes advantage of us, our first response is to hurt that person. Is this true?" Allow family members to remember incidents when people have hurt them. How did they react? Did they hit or hurt the person in return.

Continue by saying, "But loving God means that we love people also. That means when people hurt us, we should not hurt them back." (NOTE: Explain to children that this does not mean that they must endure the improper touching of adults. We can make people stop doing hurtful things to us. What the life of and teaching of Jesus reveals is a desire to free us from hate and anger toward people that hurt us. In the long run, the hate and anger may do us as much harm as the abuse.)

Closing Prayer

Allow everyone an opportunity to pray. Ask God to help us love God and love other people even people who mistreat us and try to hurt us.

Family Journal

_____
_____
_____
_____
_____
_____
_____

Thursday

If you love me, you will keep my commandments.
(John 14:15)

Scripture Reading

John 14:15-21. After the reading, you might say, "Jesus makes the whole matter very plain. The way we love him is by keeping his commandments. The word commandment may also be translated 'teaching.' What are some of the teachings of Jesus we should obey?" Allow family members to think of several. Write responses on the back of the poster board from Monday.

Review the list, item by item. You might say, "If we want to say 'I love you God,' these are the ways to say it."

Closing Prayer

Close your worship time in a few moments of silence. Ask God to help us live by the teachings of Jesus.

Family Journal

_____

_____

_____

_____

_____

_____

_____

Putting Faith into Action!

Pick one item from the list your family has made of ways to say "I love you" to God. Working as a family, actually do whatever you choose from the list. The item may be as simple as attending church together on Sunday or working at a rescue mission on Saturday. As you complete the activity, whatever it is, pause and say, "This is our way of saying we love you, God."

Sixth Week after Easter
Theme: Living in God's Time

Scripture Readings for the Week
Psalm 47; Acts 1:1-11; Ephesians 1:15-23; Luke 24:44-53

Materials Needed
Secure a kitchen timer, an egg timer, or a clock with a visible moving second hand to use as a worship tool this week.

Monday

God has gone up with a shout. (Psalm 47:1)

Scripture Reading
Psalm 47. Use the clock or timer to talk about time. You might say, "If we are baking a cake, or if we have an appointment in another city, we must carefully watch the time. We need to know not only what time it is, but also how much time something takes and how much time is left.

"With God we may talk about three different times. Thinking about 'past time' provides us with opportunities to remember all that God has done for us in the past. In 'present time' we deal with God in the here and now. 'Future time' is the time ahead of us where we will meet God in the future.

"The psalm for today touches both past and present time for the Psalmist. In it the writer remembers what God has done and celebrates what God is doing."

Closing Prayer
Close in prayer. Ask God to help us to remember the blessings of the past and celebrate the presence of God in the present.

Family Journal

_____

_____

_____

_____

_____

_____

Tuesday

It is not for you to know the times or periods
that the Father has set by his own authority. (Acts 1:7)

Scripture Reading

Acts 1:1-11. Read the verses carefully. After the reading, you might ask, "Are these verses concerned with past, present, or future time?" Help family members think through this. The incident described happened in our past. The words were spoken in the apostles' present, but the message had to do with their future and ours.

After a time of discussion, continue by asking, "What did Jesus say about the future? (He said not to worry about it.) Does that mean we don't need to work or make preparation for the future?" (No. Jesus told his followers to pray and wait. He was preparing them by teaching them spiritual disciplines.) Continue by saying, "Jesus did not say that we should ignore the future or be lazy about its coming. Rather, he said 'don't be afraid of tomorrow.' This is still good advice for us today."

Closing Prayer

Close your time of worship. Thank God for the past, present, and even the future. Pray that we might enter the future without being afraid.

Family Journal

_____
_____
_____
_____
_____
_____
_____

Wednesday

Not only in this age but also in the age to come.
(Ephesians 1:21)

Scripture Reading

Ephesians 1:15-23. After the reading, turn on the kitchen timer, or turn over the egg timer, or simply call attention to the sweeping second hand on the clock. You might say something like, "God is able to be in all three times at once. God is in the past, the present, and the future all at the same time. Therefore, God is able to work in the present, knowing what lies ahead in the future. That is why Jesus tells us not to fear the future.

"The writer of Ephesians also shares this important view of time. God is at work in past time and future time to bring about blessings and hope in present time. Because of God's special standing in time, we are able to enjoy a full and rich life right now! And the future is secure as well."

Closing Prayer

Close your worship time in prayer. Thank God for giving us this moment and filling it with memories of the past and longings for the future.

Family Journal

_____
_____
_____
_____
_____
_____

Thursday

Stay here in the city until you have been clothed with power from on high. (Luke 24:49)

Scripture Reading

Luke 24:44-53. Begin by saying, "We need to discuss one more element of time. We might call this idea of time the place where past, present, and future all come together. It is called 'timing'." Read the verses from Luke. Emphasize the wait until . . .

"Jesus had important work for his followers to do, but he told them to wait for the right moment until they were fully prepared. This is good advice for all of us. There are many things we would like to do and should do with our lives, but we may not be able to do them until the timing is right. That might mean finishing school or simply gaining more life experience.

"As we wait in God's present, we learn from the past and the present. Together these two times prepare us for the future. And when the time is right, God will send us out into the world to do our work. Meanwhile, we wait."

Closing Prayer

Close your worship time in prayer. Ask God to prepare us to live in the present and in the future.

Family Journal

_____
_____
_____
_____
_____
_____

Putting Faith into Action!

Plan something that requires careful attention to time. You may want to make an appointment to see someone or bake something that requires careful timing. Work as a family to make careful note of the use of time.

Week of Pentecost
Theme: The Work of the Holy Spirit

Scripture Readings for the Week
Psalm 104:24-35b; Acts 2:1-21; 1 Corinthians 12:3-13; John 20:19-23

Materials Needed
You will need an electric fan or something else to move air (If a fan is not available, make a fan by gluing paper to a stick).

Monday

When you send forth your spirit, they are created.
(Psalm 104:30)

Scripture Reading
Psalm 104:24-35. Before the reading, briefly explain the significance of Pentecost. This is the time in the church year when we celebrate the coming of the Holy Spirit.

Emphasize Psalm 104:30 as you read. Turn on the fan and allow everyone to feel the air move. You might say, "Even though we cannot see the air moving, we can feel it moving and know that it is there.

"The same is true of the Spirit of God. We cannot see God. God's Spirit is not visible to us.

We can, however, tell where the Spirit of God has been." Read the psalm again. Encourage family members to listen for ways the Psalmist knows where the Spirit of God has moved.

Continue by saying, "We are surrounded by reminders that God is near to us. God's Spirit moves in our world like wind."

Closing Prayer
Join hands and invite family members to pray in their own words. Thank God for making our world and for continuing to be present in our lives.

Family Journal
_____
_____
_____
_____
_____
_____

Tuesday

All of them were filled with the Holy Spirit and began to speak in other languages, as the Spirit gave them ability. (Acts 2:4)

Scripture Reading

Acts 2:1-21. Turn the fan on again. As you read, emphasize 2:3. After the reading you might say something like, "This story in the book of Acts describes the birth of the church and the coming of God's Spirit. It is important to notice that the Spirit touched each person. This means that God shares God's self with each and every one of us. I do not have more than you, or you more than me. We all equally share in the blessing of God's Spirit."

If possible, move the fan around the room. Let the air blow across the face of each family member. Continue by saying, "God has not left anyone out. All who seek God's presence in Jesus Christ receive the presence of God through the Holy Spirit. Through the Spirit of God, we are encouraged and enabled to serve God and others."

Closing Prayer

Close in prayer. Thank God for making us part of the people of God and for sharing with all of us the Holy Spirit.

Family Journal

_____
_____
_____
_____
_____
_____

Wednesday

Now there are varieties of gifts, but the same Spirit. (1 Corinthians 12:4)

Scripture Reading

1 Corinthians 12:3-13. As you move the fan around, allow each family member to name his/her favorite color and food. After the Scripture Reading, you might say, "Because the Spirit of God is given to every member of God's family, we are tempted to believe that God wants us all to be the same. In other words, the same Spirit should mold us and shape us the same way.

"But in fact the opposite is true. The presence of God does not shape us all to be the same. Instead, we are enabled by God's Spirit to develop many different gifts and skills. God works through our differences to create a family of people that work together to make God's presence known in the world."

Closing Prayer

Thank God for making us all different. Be sure to express thanksgiving for God's presence in our lives through the Spirit.

Family Journal

_____

_____

_____

_____

_____

_____

Thursday

When he had said this, he breathed on them and said to them, "Receive the Holy Spirit." (John 20:22)

Scripture Reading

John 20:19-23. After the reading, you might say, "It may seem a little confusing to us to read about Jesus breathing on his disciples and saying 'receive the Holy Spirit.' Earlier in the week we read in Acts how the Spirit descended on the Day of Pentecost. So when did the Spirit come? What is the meaning of this incident?"

Turn the fan on everybody again. Continue by saying, "Jesus was doing what we've been doing with the fan. He was trying to help his disciples understand that the Spirit would come like a breeze or even a mighty wind. He was

making a promise a promise that was kept on the Day of Pentecost that the Spirit of God would come."

Closing Prayer

Tell everyone to close their eyes. Move the fan about so that the air blows across the face of each person. Close your worship time in prayer. Thank God for sending the Spirit to help us.

Family Journal

_____

_____

_____

_____

_____

_____

Putting Faith into Action!

We learned this week that God does not make us all the same. We are different and have different gifts. Spend some time discovering what your gift is. Parents, help children understand this by sharing with them special skills or talents you have. How do these gifts serve other people?

Trinity Sunday
Theme: The Trinity

Scripture Readings for the Week
Psalm 8; Genesis 1:1 2:4a; 2 Corinthians 13:11-13;
Matthew 28:16-20

Materials Needed
Understanding the Trinity is very difficult. Almost any illustration will obscure as much as it reveals. With this in mind, use the fan from last week's worship activities to remind us of the presence of God through the Holy Spirit. Provide paper and crayons for everyone.

Monday

O LORD, our Sovereign, how majestic
is your name in all the earth! (Psalm 8:9)

Scripture Reading
Psalm 8. Before reading the psalm, turn on the fan. You might say something like, "The fan reminds us that God's Spirit meets with us as we worship." Distribute the paper and crayons to everyone. Tell family members to trace their hands on the paper. Write their name at the bottom of the page with the words, "God's hands made my hands." Read the psalm.

Continue by saying, "The Psalmist sang a song of praise to God. He looked at the earth and sky and knew that God must be very powerful. As the Psalmist thought about all the things God's hands have made, he may have looked at his own hands. Seeing how small they were in comparison, the Psalmist asked 'What are human beings that God should notice them.' Then he answered his own question: 'God has made us just a little lower than God. We are crowned with glory any honor.'

"Even though God is Spirit and we are flesh, God still loves us. God made us and values us. When we look at our hands and realize how small we are compared to God, that does not mean God cannot see us. God loves us and is near to us all the time."

Closing Prayer
Close your worship time in prayer. Thank God for creating us and loving us as we are.

Family Journal

_____
_____
_____
_____
_____
_____

Tuesday

God saw everything . . . and indeed, it was very good.
(Genesis 1:31)

Scripture Reading

Genesis 1:1 2:4. This is a long reading. If you have children old enough to read, you may want to share the reading with other family members. If not, read it with feeling and dramatic emotion. Be sure to emphasize the recurring refrain, "God saw that it was good," and in regard to the fulfillment of creation, "It was very good" (2:31).

Make sure the fan is on. The opening verses tell us that God's Spirit was blowing across the waters like a storm. After the reading you might ask, "Was God pleased with creation? (God was pleased.) How do we know God was pleased?" (We know God was pleased because over and over again God said, It is good.)

Continue by saying, "Sometimes people are tempted to believe that God does not love us or creation. Because humans do bad things, some people think God has given up on us, but that is not true. God knew when we were born that we would make mistakes. God also knew that because we are weak and have limited knowledge of things, we would hurt ourselves and other people. In spite of all that, God loves us. God does not despise our flesh because God is Spirit. God made us flesh and loves us as we are. We may not always act 'good.' But God views us as a good creation and certainly worth saving."

Closing Prayer

Close your worship time in prayer. Thank God for creating the world and placing us in it.

Family Journal

_____
_____
_____
_____
_____
_____

Wednesday

The grace of the Lord Jesus Christ, the love of God, and the communion of the Holy Spirit be with all of you.
(2 Corinthians 13:13)

Scripture Reading

2 Corinthians 13:11-13. Turn on the fan and review the hand pictures from Monday. As you read the verses from 2 Corinthians, be sure to emphasize 13:13.

After the reading, you might say something like, "The Apostle Paul closed this letter to his friends in Corinth with a very interesting arrangement of words and ideas. He said, 'The grace of the Lord Jesus Christ, the love of God, and the communion of the Holy Spirit be with all of you.' Are these three separate things? Haven't we learned that the Holy Spirit is the Spirit of God, the very presence of God? And didn't we learn that Jesus was God made flesh? So why did Paul speak in this way?

"Throughout history God has reached out to us in many different ways. God reaches out to us with the spoken and written word. God reaches out with the miracle of creation. God ultimately reached out to us through Jesus Christ. In Jesus, God touched our flesh. God finally reached out to us through the Holy Spirit.

"Remember the psalm from Monday? We are made just a little lower than God, but we are still different from God. God is Spirit, and we are flesh. Therefore, God has taken steps to overcome our differences. As a God of love, gracious savior, and daily companion through the Spirit, God touches us and offers us life."

Closing Prayer

Join hands and invite family members into a few moments of silence. Thank God for meeting us in our weakness and flesh and offering us life.

Family Journal

_____
_____
_____
_____
_____
_____

Thursday

And remember, I am with you always, to the end of the age. (Matthew 28:20)

Scripture Reading

Matthew 28:16-20. After the reading, you might say something like, "These final words of Jesus set the stage for our work and lives as followers. Jesus wants us to help all the people of the world find the peace and joy of salvation. According to Jesus, that is accomplished by teaching all people to be Christians, and then baptizing them into the full experience of God as Father, Son, and Holy Spirit. What does that mean?

"Well, what have we learned? We have learned that God is present in creation, but also distant. We have learned that God does not hate our flesh. In fact, God became flesh in Jesus the Son. Finally, we have learned that God is Spirit and chooses to be with us as we live our lives.

"It is not so important that we understand this as it is we experience it. If we can live our lives in the full awareness that God is with us, in our lives and in the world, we will be able to live lives full of meaning and joy."

Closing Prayer

Close your worship time by celebrating in prayer, and maybe even in song, the love of God that saves us and stays with us.

Family Journal

_____

_____

_____

_____

_____

_____

_____

Putting Faith into Action!

Spend the day at a local park or playground. Enjoy God's creation. If you see any trash, pick it up. Stop every once in a while and feel the wind on your face. Notice the trees moving in the breeze. Feel the warm sunshine. God is present. Try to make a new friend while you are there; God does not want us lonely.

Notes

[1]If your church observes Transfiguration Sunday as the end of Epiphany this week of activities will help your family prepare for this worship event.

[2]This week should lead up to Palm Sunday.

[3]Many churches observe every day of Holy Week with either a morning watch or evening services. The home worship activities may easily be incorporated into you family's participation in events of your church. Creatively adapt the lessons in any way that magnifies the significance of this important week.

Ordinary Time

Maintain justice, and do what is right, for soon my salvation will come, and my deliverance be revealed. Isaiah 56:1

Ordinary time is the last and longest season of the church year. The focus is on "growth" in the Christian's life and "discipleship." Commitment to the mission of the church in the world is renewed.

Proper 4[1]
Theme: The Storms of Life

Scripture Readings for the Week
Psalm 46; Genesis 6:9-22; 7:24; 8:14-19; Romans 1:16-17; 3:22b-28; Matthew 7:21-29

Materials Needed
Make a tornado in a jar. Fill a jar nearly full of water. Add several drops of food coloring (any dark color will work). Secure the lid on tightly. Hold the top and bottom of the jar firmly. Move the jar in a vigorous circular motion. The water inside will swirl, creating a tiny tornado in a jar.

Monday

God is our refuge and strength,
a very present help in trouble. (Psalm 46:1)

Scripture Reading
Psalm 46. After the reading, show everyone the tornado in a jar. You might say something like, "Tornadoes are terrible storms that can do great damage, but tornadoes are not the only dangerous thing in our world. The Psalmist named several dangers. What are some of the dangers mentioned?" Allow family members time to think of some. Read the psalm again.

Continue by saying, "Storms and hard times touch everyone sooner or later. What does the Psalmist do when faced with tough times?" (The Psalmist finds safety and protection in God.) Spend a few moments talking about tough times your family has had, or may have. There may be sick relatives or other major changes coming in the near future.

Closing Prayer
After discussing these issues, spend some time in prayer. Ask God to help us as we face our own storms in life.

Family Journal
_____
_____
_____
_____
_____
_____
_____

Tuesday

But I will establish my covenant with you. (Genesis 6:18)

Scripture Reading

Genesis 6:9-22. Have some fun with the Noah story. Let your children tell you the story instead of reading to them. After the reading or telling, pick up on the theme of storms again. This storm lasted a long time and changed everything.

Continue by saying, "Sometimes when we are going through a storm we may start thinking that the storm will never end. We can become so frightened that we give up hope. The story of Noah and his storm serves to remind us that God gives hope even in the storm" (read 6:18-22).

Closing Prayer

Close your worship time in prayer. Offer God thanks for going through the storms with us. Ask God to give us hope in the midst of the storms.

Family Journal

_____
_____
_____
_____
_____
_____

Wednesday

All have sinned and fall short of the glory of God; they are now justified by his grace as a gift.
(Romans 3:23-24)

Scripture Reading

Romans 1:16-17; 3:22-28. After the reading, make the tornado in the jar. Continue by saying, "Not all the storms we face are storms outside. Some of the storms we face are inside in our hearts and minds. For example, if I do something I know I am not supposed to do, I will feel a terrible feeling of guilt. The longer we carry that feeling, the worse it becomes. Pretty soon, the guilt in me is like a storm inside my head. It can even make me sick.

"In the verses we read from Romans, Paul describes how everyone has a storm of guilt. 'Everyone sins,' he said, 'and falls short of the glory of God.' In that fall is a storm of bad feelings, but God offers hope even in the storms that blow through our lives. God offers us forgiveness from our guilt. All we have to do is ask and God will forgive us."

Closing Prayer

Close your worship time in prayer. Ask God to help us with the storms we stir up in our lives by doing things that we know are wrong. Pray for God's forgiveness.

Family Journal

_____
_____
_____
_____
_____

Thursday

Everyone then who hears these words of mine and acts on them will be like a wise man who built his house on rock. (Matthew 7:24)

Scripture Reading

Matthew 7:21-29. After the reading, you might say something like, "This week we have looked at two kinds of storms. There are storms outside such as tornadoes and major changes in our lives and there are storms inside.

"Jesus knew about these storms. In the verses we read today, Jesus tells us how to prepare for the storms of life. If we build our lives on a solid foundation of truth, when the storms come, we can weather them (get through them). Notice that Jesus does not say if the storms come. He says when the storms come. Storms come to everyone sooner or later. Let's be ready."

Closing Prayer

Ask God to help us build our lives on a strong foundation a foundation of truth. Ask God to help us when the storms come.

Family Journal

_____
_____
_____
_____
_____

Putting Faith into Action!

Late Spring and early Summer brings volatile weather to many parts of the country. Look around your neighborhood. Do you have neighbors or friends who are vulnerable to storms because of age or other physical factors. Visit these folks and see if you can help them prepare for future storms.

How about your own family? Do you have a storm plan? What do you do in the event of a fire? Where does everybody go? What do we do if bad weather comes? Do you have a plan? If not, form one.

Proper 5[2]
Theme: Mercy, Sacrifice, and Keeping the Rules

Scripture Readings for the Week
Psalm 50:7-15; Hosea 5:15 6:6; Romans 4:13-25;
Matthew 9:9-13, 18-26

Materials Needed
Arrange chairs to simulate the inside of your car.

Monday

Offer to God a sacrifice of thanksgiving,
and pay your vows to the Most High. (Psalm 50:14)

Scripture Reading
Psalm 50:7-15. Play an imaginary game with family members called "Going to Church." Allow everyone to call out things they see on the way to church. After a few minutes, you might say, "Oh my. There is someone injured on the side of the road. We should stop and help them. Oh no, look at the time. If we stop and help, we'll be late for church. God wants us in church, so we better not stop." Allow family members to express their feelings about your decision.

After the game, read the psalm. Emphasize 50:14-15. You might ask, "Did I do the right thing to leave an injured person on the side of the road? Was I right to think that God cared more about us being at the church on time than about a hurting person? The Psalmist said that God wanted a 'sacrifice of thanksgiving.' How thankful are we if overlook the needs of others?"

Closing Prayer
Allow everyone an opportunity to pray. Ask God to remind us that our blessings are opportunities to help others.

Family Journal
_____
_____
_____
_____
_____
_____

Tuesday

For I desire steadfast love and not sacrifice,
the knowledge of God rather than burnt offerings.
(Hosea 6:6)

Scripture Reading

Hosea 5:15 6:6. Emphasize Hosea 6:6. After the reading, you might say something like, "The ancient Hebrews thought that God wanted them to faithfully sacrifice animals at the temple. They thought this would please God, but the prophets like Hosea told the people that true worship was not a matter of piling dead animals on an altar. True worship was a matter of showing love."

Talk about the "Going to Church Game." You might say, "God does want us to go to church, but the purpose of going to church is to encourage us to show love to people. If we drive past someone who is hurting in an effort to get to church, we defeat the purpose of going to church in the first place."

Closing Prayer

Close your worship time in prayer. Ask God to help love each other and be willing to offer help to others in need.

Family Journal

_____

_____

_____

_____

Wednesday

Therefore his faith was reckoned
to him as righteousness. (Romans 4:22)

Scripture Reading

Romans 4:13-25. This will be a hard reading for children. The best way to make it clear will be to paraphrase it in your own words. Here is one example: "Abraham did not become a great man of God because he kept all the rules and never made a mistake. Pleasing God is not about keeping a bunch of rules. Pleasing God is about loving God and having a real friendship with God. Abraham trusted God, loved God, followed God, and took chances with God. Because Abraham trusted God, God called him a righteous man. It was not the rule keeping that made Abraham righteous, it was God's love and grace."

After the reading and/or paraphrase, you might say something like, "Anyone who would drive by an injured person because they were late for church is someone who believes that God cares more about the rules than about people. God wants us to be good people and not do bad things, but if we neglect people in the process, we miss the point."

Closing Prayer

Instruct family members to spend a few moments in silent prayer. Close in prayer by asking God to help us know how to live lives that are good, but that are also helpful.

Family Journal

_____

_____

_____

Thursday

Go and learn what this means,
"I desire mercy, not sacrifice." (Matthew 9:13)

Scripture Reading

Matthew 9:9-13, 18-26. After the reading, you might say something like, "Jesus understood very well how God feels about the rules we come up with. The Pharisees did not want Jesus being friends with tax collectors and sinners. It was against 'their rules,' but Jesus told them what the prophets had said many times before 'God wants mercy, not rule keeping.'

"Then to illustrate his point, Jesus performed two acts of kindness (vv. 18-26). In the first case, he affirmed the faith of a woman who was seeking healing. In the second instance,

Jesus raised a little girl from the dead. Both of these 'acts of mercy' involved females. It was against the rules to have contact with sick women or dead people, but when you are showing mercy, certain rules just don't make any sense."

Closing Prayer

Close your worship time in prayer. Ask God to help us know when our rules are keeping us from showing mercy.

Family Journal

_____

_____

_____

_____

Putting Faith into Action!

Working as a family, think of someone you know who needs mercy or assistance. For example, do you know an elderly or ill person who cannot keep their yard work up. Do you know a single parent who has to work so many hours that he or she does not have time to prepare good meals? Maybe you know someone who is lonely. The Lord wants mercy shown to these people. Are there rules to keep us from doing so?

Proper 6³
Theme: How God Wants Us To Live

Scripture Readings for the Week
Psalm 100; Exodus 19:2-8a; Romans 5:1-8; Matthew 9:35 10:8

Materials Needed
Using colored construction paper for a cover and a few pages of white paper for the inside, make a small "How To" book. Have markers on hand to fill in the pages and decorate the cover as you go along.

Monday

Make a joyful noise to the LORD, all the earth.
(Psalm 100:1)

Scripture Reading
Psalm 100. Begin by saying something like, "As we worship and study this week, we are going to make a little 'How To' book. This book will be about how God wants us to live. We will start with Psalm 100.

After reading the psalm ask, "How does the Psalmist think we should live?" Allow time for responses. Read the psalm a second time if necessary. Continue by saying, "The Psalmist tells

us that we should live praising and thanking God. Let's write that in our book."

Closing Prayer
Close your worship time praising and thanking God. Ask for God's guidance as we seek to live the way God wants us to live.

Family Journal
_____
_____
_____
_____
_____
_____
_____

Tuesday

Indeed, the whole earth is mine, but you shall be for me a priestly kingdom and a holy nation.
(Exodus 19:5-6)

Scripture Reading
Exodus 19:2-8. Be sure to emphasize verse 5 as you read these verses. After the reading, you

might say, "God wants us to be special people. God's people are the people who can really make a difference in the world. God's people can help other people find God.

"In order to be God's people, however, God says there is something we must do. What is it?" Allow family members to respond. Read the verses again if needed. Continue by saying, "In order for us to live as God's people we must first be willing to obey God's commandments and honor the agreement between us. This is not just keeping the rules as we have already noticed. Obeying God means living our lives as one of God's own children. Let's write that in our book."

Closing Prayer

Join hand and invite family members to offer a prayer in their own words. Ask God to help us be the people of God in this world.

Family Journal

_____
_____
_____
_____
_____
_____
_____

Wednesday

For while we were still weak, at the right time Christ died for the ungodly. (Romans 5:6)

Scripture Reading

Romans 5:1-8. After the reading, you might say something like, "These verses in Romans are very important for teaching us how to live. Paul reminds us of two things that we must never forget. The first is that we are weak. Because we are weak from time to time, we will suffer. We must not think that suffering is a sign that God does not care for us. Suffering simply means that we are human and feel pain.

"The second thing Paul reminds us is that we were all sinners before we became believers. If we forget that we were all sinners, we might start thinking that we are better than other people. That would be a mistake. God loves all of us, and wants us to love all people. If we remember what we have in common with all people, it will help us love them."

Closing Prayer

Let's write that in our book. We all suffer. We are all sinners. We should live remembering this. Close in prayer, thanking God for helping us through our suffering and in spite of our sin.

Family Journal

_____

_____

_____

_____

_____

_____

Thursday

The harvest is plentiful, but the laborers are few.
(Matthew 9:37)

Scripture Reading

Matthew 9:35 10:8. After the reading, you might say something like, "One way we can know how God wants us to live is to pay attention to Jesus's life and words. These verses provide us with an opportunity to do just that. In verses 9:35-38, we find a description of Jesus going about doing good and preaching the kingdom of God. We also find Jesus praying for people in need. In 10:1-8, we read about Jesus sending his disciples out into the world Jesus just prayed for. The disciples were told to do good things and preach the kingdom of God.

"What do you think we should do with our lives? How should we live?" Allow family members time to respond. Read the verses again if needed. Continue by saying, "Let's write this in our 'How to Live Book.' Let's write, 'God wants us to do good things for people in need, tell people about God's love, and pray for our world.' "

Closing Prayer

Close your worship time. Pray for our world and its many needs. Ask God to use us to help meet some of those needs.

Family Journal

_____

_____

_____

_____

_____

_____

Putting Faith into Action!

We wrote four things in our "How to Live" book this week. Review them. Working as a family, try to do all the things written in your book. If they can't all be done in one day, take a couple of days to complete them. You might even want to do them everyday for the rest of your life.

Proper 7[4]
Theme: When God Feels Far Away

Scripture Readings for the Week
Psalm 69:7-10, 16-18; Jeremiah 20:7-13; Romans 6:1b-11; Matthew 10:24-39

Materials Needed
Try to find a picture of a sparrow. An encyclopedia or biology book may have one. If a picture is not available just draw one.

Monday

Draw near to me, redeem me,
set me free because of my enemies. (Psalm 69:18)

Scripture Reading
Psalm 69:7-10, 16-18. Show or draw the picture of the sparrow. Talk about how small and frail the sparrow is. Sparrows are so small that sometimes we forget they are even in the world. Read the psalm for today. You might say something like, "The person who wrote these words also felt very small. Bad things were happening in his life. People were trying to hurt him. In addition to all of this, the Psalmist felt like God was far away." Read verses 16-18. Continue by saying, "The Psalmist does not say, 'I'm glad

you're here.' Instead he says, 'Please come here right away!' "

Closing Prayer
Pain and fear can make us feel small. We might even be tempted to believe that God has overlooked us, like a small sparrow. Let us pray and ask God to help us in times of fear and pain.

Family Journal
_____
_____
_____
_____
_____
_____

Tuesday

I have become a laughingstock all day long;
everyone mocks me . . . Praise the LORD!
(Jeremiah 20:7, 13)

Scripture Reading

Jeremiah 20:7-13. After the reading, you might say something like, "The psalm we read yesterday revealed a person who felt as if God were far away. Today we read about a prophet who wishes God was far away! Why?" Allow family members to respond. Read the verses again if needed.

After a few moments of discussion, you might continue by saying, "The words Jeremiah was speaking on behalf of God were making people very unhappy. Jeremiah was being threatened. People were calling him names. Even though he was doing God's work, Jeremiah felt small and alone. That was why he called out to God."

Read again verse 13. You might say, "Even though Jeremiah felt threatened and weak, and even though his friends were turning against him, he was still able to praise God. Jeremiah, even in the midst of his pain, called upon the Lord and believed that God would help him."

Closing Prayer

Close in your time of worship in prayer. Thank God for caring about weak and needy people people like us.

Family Journal

_____
_____
_____
_____
_____
_____
_____

Wednesday

So you also must consider yourselves dead
to sin and alive to God in Christ Jesus. (Romans 6:11)

Scripture Reading

Romans 6:1-11. This will be a difficult reading for children. You might want to paraphrase the meaning of the text. Here is one example: "All around us there are powerful influences that tempt us to live in ways that are not good. Our whole world is organized around this kind of selfishness. If we are not careful, we can be pulled into things that are clearly not good for us.

"When we are baptized into Christ, God moves into our lives to help us. God tries to put to death the influence the world has on us. The more we devote ourselves to God, the less influence the world will have over us.

"In this world of power and might, we might be small and weak. We may feel like the sparrows we saw on Monday, but if God is in our lives through Jesus Christ, then we have the power to resist the world and live a life of love and thankfulness."

Closing Prayer
Invite family members to spend a few moments in prayerful silence. Thank God for giving us a way to resist the deadly influence of this world.

Family Journal

_____
_____
_____
_____
_____

Thursday

So do not be afraid; you are of more value than many sparrows. (Matthew 10:31)

Scripture Reading
Matthew 10:24-39. Before reading these verses, you might say, "Yesterday we read that God did not want us to be like the world around us. Listen to the words of Jesus today as he gives us some specific examples. Try to remember some of things he warns us about."

After the reading, call on family members to share what they heard Jesus saying. Jesus encourages us not to be afraid of people in power. If we cater to the wishes of the powerful

out of fear, we may end up not doing what pleases God. Continue by saying, "Fear makes us feel very small, like sparrows, but notice what Jesus said. If even one sparrow falls from the sky, God knows about it. How much more will God know what is happening with us?"

Closing Prayer
Ask family members to offer a prayer of thanks to God for helping us live without fear in a difficult world.

Family Journal

_____
_____
_____
_____
_____

Putting Faith into Action!

Make a list of things that frighten you. Everyone should contribute to the list. Do these frightening things make us feel like God is far away? How can we overcome our fear of these things? What can we do to make our world safer? Working as a family, address one another's fears. come up with ways to help each other feel safe and secure. Remember, God is watching you, no matter how small you may be.

Proper 8[5]
Theme: Just a Cup of Water

Scripture Readings for the Week
Psalm 13; Genesis 22:1-14; Romans 6:12-23;
Matthew 10:40-42

Materials Needed
You will need a cup of water for the worship lessons.

Monday

Consider and answer me, O LORD my God! (Psalm 13)

Scripture Reading
Psalm 13. After reading the psalm, say something like, "When we play or work hard, our body uses up a lot of water. That is why we get thirsty." Take a sip from the cup of water. Continue by saying, "Nothing is quite as refreshing and good as nice cool water when you are hot and thirsty.

"Our bodies can get dry and need water when we work hard. The same is true for our emotions, our minds, and our spirits. If we work hard with our brains trying to solve a difficult problem or doing a lot of school work, sometimes our brains get tired and we need to rest or play. Or, if we get upset over something and we are frightened or angry for a long time, our emotions may dry out and need refreshing.

"The Psalmist described going through terrible pain. The pain and worry had left him wondering where God was. This is like 'spiritual thirst.' The Psalmist was thirsty for God." Ask, "Does the Psalmist think God will eventually come and offer help?" Allow time for family members to respond.

Closing Prayer
Close your worship time by reading verses 5-6. Thank God for offering us the refreshing water of God's presence.

Family Journal

_____
_____
_____
_____
_____
_____
_____

Tuesday

So Abraham call that place "The LORD will provide."
(Genesis 22:14)

Scripture Reading

Genesis 22:1-14. (Note to parents: This is a difficult story to read or tell to children. It is not wise, however, to skip these stories only to have our children find them later and have no frame of reference for understanding them.)

Before the reading, you might say, "There was a time when people thought that God wanted human sacrifice. These people thought that God was so hard to please that only the sacrifice of a beloved child could satisfy God. Today we know that is not true." Read the passage for today. Continue by saying, "We do not know why God told Abraham to do this. The Bible says that God was testing Abraham, but it seems like a pretty hard test.

"Of course, life is hard. Maybe Abraham needed to know how much he loved his son and how much he loved God. Maybe Isaac needed to see how much Abraham trusted God. Or, maybe Abraham simply misunderstood the message. We just don't know. What we do know is that God did not allow Isaac to be harmed. God provided a sacrifice and Abraham was able to keep his son." You might ask at this point, "Does that sound familiar?" God provides a sacrifice and we are saved? Allow family members to respond.

Pass the cup of water around to every family member. Everyone should take a sip. As the cup goes around you might say, "Life is hard. It can make us dry, but the grace of God saves and refreshes us even in the midst of painful situations."

Closing Prayer

Close in your worship time in prayer. Thank God for meeting us in our tough times.

Family Journal

_____
_____
_____
_____
_____
_____

Wednesday

Present yourselves to God. (Romans 6:13)

Scripture Reading

Romans 6:12-23. This is another hard reading from Romans. You might want to paraphrase these verses. Here is one suggestion: "As we go through life we will make all kinds of sacrifices. We will give up things for an education, or a job, or even for a family. Yesterday we saw Abraham ready to give up his son in order to please God. Of course, he didn't need nor have to do this, but he was willing.

"That is the kind of thing Paul was writing about in Romans. We offer ourselves to all sorts of things, but Paul warns us to be careful. We should present ourselves to God rather than to behaviors that are not good. If we present ourselves to bad things, we will do bad things. If we present ourselves to God, God will help us to become the kind of people God wants us to be."

Pass the water cup around again. Continue by saying, "It is like this cup of water. If we drink dirty water, full of germs, we will get sick. But if we drink clear, clean water, we will be healthy. Let us drink the good water of God's love."

Closing Prayer

Close in your worship time in prayer. Ask God to help us present ourselves to God rather than to other things in our world.

Family Journal

_____
_____
_____
_____
_____
_____
_____

Thursday

Truly I tell you, none of these
will lose their reward. (Matthew 10:42)

Scripture Reading

Matthew 10:40-42. After the reading, you might say, "Jesus understood the importance of water very well. We might think that God is only pleased when we do really great and wonderful things, but that is not true. Even the little things we do please God. If we just offer someone a drink of water, but we do it out of love and concern, God considers that a great thing. God would call us a prophet! Why do you think this is true?" Allow family members time to reflect and respond.

Continue by saying, "If the things we do, both large and small, are motivated by our love for God, then God is pleased. One of the reasons God refreshes us and saves us is so we can help make God known to others. If all we ever do is offer some water, that is important."

Closing Prayer

Thank God for noticing even the little things we do. Be sure to express thanksgiving for God's presence in our lives.

Family Journal

_____

_____

_____

_____

_____

_____

_____

Putting Faith into Action!

Anybody doing yard work or construction in your neighborhood this weekend? Any big work days at the church? Is there a road crew digging up the highway in front of your house? Make a big pitcher of ice water or lemonade. Offer these hard working people a cool, refreshing drink. God will be there.

Proper 9⁶
Theme: Learning To Be Humble

Scripture Readings for the Week
Psalm 145:8-14; Zechariah 9:9-12; Romans 7:15-25a;
Matthew 11: 25-30

Materials Needed
You will need a hand held mirror for this week.

Monday

Your kingdom is an everlasting kingdom. (Psalm 145:13)

Scripture Reading
Psalm 145:8-14. Emphasize verse 13 as you read this psalm. After the reading, pass the mirror around for everyone to look at. Of course, everyone will be looking at their own reflection. When the mirror comes back to you, hold it away from you so that family members can still see their reflection.

You might say something like, "There are two mistakes we make about ourselves. We tend to either think too highly of ourselves or we think too little of ourselves. We are either self centered or we don't like ourselves. Both attitudes are wrong.

"God wants us to be honest about ourselves. We don't need to act more important than we are. After all, God is king! At the same time, we should not think too lowly of ourselves. Even if we have made mistakes in life, God still loves us. God loves the lowly."

Closing Prayer
Let each family member take another look in the mirror. As a family say, God loves you when each person looks in the mirror. Close your worship time in prayer. Thank God for loving us just as we are.

Family Journal
_____
_____
_____
_____
_____
_____
_____

Tuesday

Lo, your king comes to you; triumphant and victorious is he, humble and riding on a donkey.
(Zechariah 9:9)

Scripture Reading

Zechariah 9:9-12. After the reading, you might say something like, "We are often impressed by strength. Huge tanks, missiles, big guns, and fast airplanes are all symbols of power and might. People who work out and have huge muscles are admired for their strength. Look in the mirror. Are we strong or weak?

"God tells us that our king will ride humbly into our lives on the back of donkey. God is not impressed with our strength. God knows that when we are bragging about how strong we are we are really very frightened by how weak we are.

"Jesus came into our lives as a humble king. He invites us to embrace ourselves as weak, humble persons, and follow a humble king. Jesus offers us a way around the temptation to be strong. Strength only brings violence and death, but humble love brings hope and peace."

Closing Prayer

Allow each family member an opportunity to pray. Ask God to help us not trust in our own strength, but to live out of our weakness and humility in Christ.

Family Journal

_____
_____
_____
_____
_____
_____
_____

Wednesday

So then, with my mind I am a slave to the law of God, but with my flesh I am a slave to the law of sin.
(Romans 7:25)

Scripture Reading

Romans 7:15-25. These verses in Romans are pretty clear. Allow family members to struggle with them. After the reading, you might ask, "Is Paul admitting strength or weakness with these words? Does Paul sound humble or proud?" Allow family members to discuss for a while.

Continue by saying, "One way we become truly humble is by being honest with ourselves and with others. If we pretend to be something we are not, we are admitting that we are not humble. If we say openly and plainly that we struggle with things, then we recognize our humble standing before God. That is what Paul does in these verses."

Closing Prayer

Look in the mirror. Can we be honest with ourselves and honest with God about who we are? If we can, God will be able to use us and help us. Close in prayer. Ask God to help us be truthful about our lives.

Family Journal

_____

_____

_____

_____

_____

_____

_____

Thursday

For my yoke is easy, and my burden is light.
(Matthew 11:30)

Scripture Reading

Matthew 11:25-30. After the scripture reading, you might say something like, "It takes a lot of effort to pretend to be something we are not. If we are trying to act tough or smart or witty, it takes a lot of effort. Being something we are not makes us tired.

"Jesus knew this. He invites us to stop pretending. Jesus invites us to follow him and to do his work. Jesus did not try to impress anyone. He didn't try to fool people about his strength and weaknesses. He said of himself, 'I am gentle and humble in heart.' He invites us to share that humility and gentleness in our own lives. Look in the mirror. What do you see? What does God see? Can we be humble and gentle?"

Closing Prayer

Close in your time of worship in prayer. Ask God to help us accept Jesus' invitation to follow him and learn from him.

Family Journal

_____

_____

_____

_____

_____

_____

_____

Putting Faith into Action!

Think of someone the whole family knows and regards as a humble person. This person might be a school teacher, a minister, or a public official. The person might work in the service industry as a cook or waitress. You decide. After selecting a person you all know, invite that person to your home for a meal. Tell the person you just wanted to say thanks.

Proper 10[7]
Theme: The Word of God and the Human Heart

Scripture Readings for the Week
Psalm 119:105-112; Isaiah 55:10-13; Romans 8:1-11;
Matthew 13:1-9, 18-23

Materials Needed
Secure a Bible, seeds of some kind, and a drawing of the human heart.

Monday

Your word is a lamp to my feet
and a light to my path. (Psalm 119:105)

Scripture Reading
Psalm 119:105-112. After the reading, hold up the Bible and the picture of the heart. You might say something like, "The writers of the Bible talked about the 'Word of God' a little differently than we do. When we talk about the Word of God, we think immediately of the Bible. The Bible is the word of God, but the Psalmist, for example, limited the Word of God to the Law of Moses. The 'Word' that the Psalmist refers to over and over again in Psalm 119 is the Ten Commandments and other covenant instruction.

"The Word of God and the human heart are also closely linked. To writers of the Bible, the heart was the place where people reasoned and made decisions. Therefore, if a person put the Word of God into his or her heart, it would change the way that person thought and acted. Light changes the way a path looks in the dark in a similar way."

Closing Prayer
Read the passage again. Encourage family members to listen for the word heart. Close your worship time. Ask God to help us follow and learn from God's Word how we should live.

Family Journal
_____
_____
_____
_____
_____
_____

Tuesday

. . . so shall my word be that goes out of my mouth.
(Isaiah 55:11)

Scripture Reading

Isaiah 55:10-13. After the reading, you might say, "The Psalmist thought of the Word of God as light for the heart. The prophet, however, thinks of the Word of God as seeds for the heart. Show everyone the seeds and the picture of the heart.

Continue by saying, "What do seeds do? (They grow!) For the prophet, getting the Word of God into someone's heart was a way of encouraging people to study and reflect on the Word of God. God changes us from the inside out by growing Gods' Word in us."

Closing Prayer

Allow everyone an opportunity to pray. Ask God to plant the seeds of the Word of God in our hearts. Pray that it will grow there and help us.

Family Journal

_____

_____

_____

_____

_____

_____

_____

Wednesday

But you are not in the flesh; you are in the Spirit,
since the Spirit of God dwells in you. (Romans 8:9)

Scripture Reading

Romans 8:1-11. After the reading, you might say something like, "Paul does not use the word heart in these verses, but he could have. The word that is translated 'mind' could just have easily been heart." You may want to paraphrase the rest of it. Here is one suggestion:

"All people who have Jesus in their hearts are free from blame and guilt. God sets us free from the power of sin in our minds. The more we seek to fill our minds with the truths of Jesus, the easier it will be for us to live the kind of life God chooses for us.

"This is not an easy battle. Because we are still flesh and blood humans we are easily tempted to resort to our old ways. We must constantly fill our hearts with the truth of God's love and hope for us."

Closing Prayer

Close in your time of worship in prayer. Ask God to help us open our minds and hearts to the truth of the Word of God found in Jesus.

Family Journal

_____
_____
_____
_____
_____
_____
_____

Thursday

But as for what was sown on good soil, this is the one who hears the word and understands it, who indeed bears fruit.
(Matthew 13:23)

Scripture Reading

Matthew 13:1-9, 18-23. After the reading, show everyone the heart and seeds. Continue by saying, "Jesus also used the heart and seed idea to talk about God's Word. Jesus helps us understand how easy it is for the Word of God to miss its mark. If the heart is not ready, if its hard, or if it is thinking about other things, the Word will have a hard time taking root and growing.

"Where there is a willing heart (soft soil) however, then the seed of the Word of God can find a place to root in and bring a great harvest." Ask, "How can we be sure that we have our hearts ready for the Word of God?" Work with family members to come up with several suggestions.

Closing Prayer

Ask God to put the Word of God in our hearts and let it grow there until it becomes a great harvest in our lives.

Family Journal

_____
_____
_____
_____
_____
_____

Putting Faith into Action!

Take the seeds you have used all week and plant them in a flower pot. Call the flower pot your Family Heart Pot. As the seeds take root and grow, remind each other that Word of God is also growing in our hearts.

Proper 11⁸
Theme: Living In a World of Evil

Scripture Readings for the Week
Psalm 86:11-17; Genesis 28:10-19a; Romans 8:12-25; Matthew 13:24-30; 36-43

Materials Needed
Collect some blades of grass and a few weeds for your worship tools.

Monday

Give me an undivided heart to revere your name.
(Psalm 86:11)

Scripture Reading
Psalm 86:11-17. Before the reading, show everyone the grass and the weeds. You might say something like, "Our world is very much like a yard. It is made up of grass and weeds. The grass is what we want there the good things in life. The weeds are what we don't want there the evil things in life. As we go through life we must learn how to face the good and the bad."

Read Psalm 86:11-17. After the reading, ask, "Where does evil come from in this psalm? (From evil men who make threats against the Psalmist.) Where is the good?" (The good is in the Psalmist calling on the Lord to help him. There is also good in the hope that God will help him.) Continue by saying, "One of the ways we learn to deal with evil is to ask the Lord to help us. It is difficult to wait sometimes for a painful situation to end, but if we wait, not only will the pain end, but we will see God in the process."

Closing Prayer
Close your worship time in a few moments of silence. Thank God for helping us face a difficult world of pain and evil.

Family Journal
_____
_____
_____
_____
_____
_____
_____

Tuesday

*Surely the LORD is in this place
and I did not know it! (Genesis 28:16)*

Scripture Reading

Genesis 28:10-19. Before reading the verses from Genesis, briefly review the events in Jacob's life leading up to this moment. It is hard to untangle all the bad choices that were made both on Jacob's part and Esau's part. The point at which this incident begins, however, is Jacob isolated and driven away from his home.

Read Genesis 28:10-19. Continue by saying, "Sometimes evil results from things other people do to us. Other times evil results from things we have done. If our actions are involved, we might be tempted to believe that God is through with us.

"That may be how Jacob felt. Perhaps he felt cut off and isolated from God. Maybe he felt like evil circumstances had driven God away from him. Maybe he felt totally alone. If he did, then his dream was a powerful lesson for him to learn. No matter how bad things may get on earth, God always keeps a way open to get to us and offer us help and blessing."

Closing Prayer

Close your worship time in prayer. Ask God to help us see where the openings are. Ask God to keep us from believing that God has left us.

Family Journal

_____
_____
_____
_____
_____
_____
_____

Wednesday

I consider that the sufferings of this present time are not worth comparing with the glory about to be revealed to us. (Romans 8:18)

Scripture Reading

Romans 8:12-25. After the reading, you might say something like, "So far we have seen that evil comes from people. It may be people doing something to us, or it may be us doing things we know are not right. The fact is, much evil and suffering results from what we do, but evil also comes from another source. Paul writes that the whole world is subject to decay. From that decay suffering and evil result. Because our world wears out, we have floods, earthquakes, and volcanoes. Our wearing out world is also responsible for germs, bacteria, and viruses. How can we live in a world that seems to be organized against us?

"Paul writes that God made the world the way it is. God made it so that it would wear out to show us that God does not wear out. We are promised comfort and blessing that is far greater than the suffering that results from a wearing out world." Allow time for questions. These discussions of suffering, death, and evil, may raise some tender questions from family members. Allow time for feelings to be expressed.

Closing Prayer
Join hands and invite family members to pray in their own words. Thank God for offering us hope in a world that is wearing out.

Family Journal

_____

_____

_____

_____

_____

_____

_____

Thursday

Explain to us the parable of the weeds of the field.
(Matthew 13:36)

Scripture Reading
Matthew 13:24-30, 36-43. After the reading, you might say something like, "Jesus puts the whole good and evil question into a simple story of weeds and grass. His story helps us understand two very important ideas about this question. First of all, only the good will survive. Whatever is evil, will be like weeds bundled together and burned. That means if we are involved in doing evil things, they will not last. If we are involved in doing good things, however, they will last forever.

"The second important idea this story teaches us is this: God will not allow evil to win out. Evil may look like it is growing and even taking over the good, but the story promises that it will not. That means that no matter how difficult our world may look from time to time, we can have confidence to do the right thing. We can also have hope that God will win in the end."

Closing Prayer
Close you worship time in prayer. Thank God for telling us the truth about evil. Ask God to help us to have hope and to not be afraid.

Family Journal

_____
_____
_____
_____
_____
_____
_____

Putting Faith into Action!

Sit down with the a newspaper or watch the news together. You won't have to watch or read very far before seeing some examples of evil. Talk about how it makes you feel? Are there evil events in the world we contribute to? Are there painful events in the world where we might offer help and seek to alleviate suffering to some degree?

Proper 12⁹
Theme: The Real Treasures of Life

Scripture Readings for the Week
Psalm 119:129-136; 1 Kings 3:5-12; Romans 8:26-39; Matthew 13: 31-33, 44-52

Materials Needed
You will need a jewelry box.

Monday

How can young people keep their way pure? By guarding it according to your word. (Psalm 119:9)

Scripture Reading
Psalm 119:129-136. After the reading, you might say something like, "This jewelry box was made to keep important and valuable items. It is like a little treasure box. The Psalmist describes his soul as a treasure box for God's word. The Psalmist writes, 'Your decrees are wonderful; therefore my soul keeps them.'

"We may own many valuable and important possessions as we go through life. We will want to keep them safe, but we must also learn how to know what is truly valuable. The words of God, and the things God wants us to do, are very valuable. Where will we keep these?"

Closing Prayer
In our souls, in our minds, and in our hearts this is where God's treasure is kept. Close your worship time in prayer. Ask God to build a treasure chest in your life.

Family Journal
_____
_____
_____
_____
_____
_____
_____

Tuesday

Give your servant therefore an understanding mind . . . able to discern between good and evil. (1 Kings 3:9)

Scripture Reading
1 Kings 3:5-12. Before the reading, you might say, "Pretend for a moment that this jewelry box was filled with all the most expensive diamonds and rubies in the world. Now imagine

that God said you could have anything in the world you wanted. What would you ask for?"

Before allowing any responses, read 1 Kings 3:5-12. Continue by asking, "What did Solomon ask for? Did his request please God? Why?" Allow time for discussion of each question. Say, "We may never ever get a chance to make a wish come true the way Solomon did. However, we will make decisions about what we will work for in life, and what our dreams will be. We will be tempted to choose the same things Solomon could have wished for: power, wealth, or youth. If we work for understanding, and wisdom, our lives will be full and rich in other ways."

Closing Prayer

Close in prayer. Ask God to give us understanding, and wisdom for the living of our lives.

Family Journal

_____
_____
_____
_____
_____
_____
_____

Wednesday

Who will separate us from the love of Christ?
(Romans 8:35)

Scripture Reading

Romans 8:26-39. After the reading, you might say something like, "One of the great treasures of life is people. The people in our lives provide joy, companionship, and support. God is very aware of the importance of people.

"That is why the Bible is filled with family images. God is portrayed as 'Parent.' Other Christians are referred to as 'brother' and 'sister.' In these verses in Romans, Paul described the process whereby we become members of God's family. That family relationship is a treasure. From the safety and security of this relationship we are able to experience the love of Christ and face the difficulties of the world."

Closing Prayer

Close your worship time in prayer. Thank God for including us in the family of God.

Family Journal

_____
_____
_____
_____
_____
_____

Thursday

Again, the kingdom of heaven is like . . . (Matthew 13:45)

Scripture Reading

Matthew 13:31-33, 44-52. After the reading, you might say, "Jesus spoke often about the kingdom of God. The kingdom of God means living with God in charge. When God is in charge of our lives, we are in the family of God. We will also do things the way God wants them done. God, however, does not force us to obey. We are invited, not commanded.

"That is why Jesus told these parables about what it would look like with God in charge. In nearly every instance, the kingdom was compared to some kind of treasure. In fact, Jesus said, letting God be in charge was like finding a great treasure in a field. We would do anything to have it.

"That is how we must approach our relationship with God. God is in charge. When we let God be in charge of our lives, then we find the true treasure of life."

Closing Prayer

Close in the time of worship in a few moments of silence. Ask God to help us make good choices, and to always choose to let God be in charge.

Family Journal

_____
_____
_____
_____
_____
_____
_____

Putting Faith into Action!

Go on a treasure hunt. You might want to hide something in your own yard. Draw maps and leave clues. Provide a special prize to the winner. Another option would be to go on another kind of Treasure Hunt. Visit a library or museum. Visit a nursing home or hospital. Visit a rescue mission or shelter for homeless persons. These are treasures? Yes.

Proper 13[10]
Theme: Bread for the Hungry

Scripture Readings for the Week
Psalm 145:8-9, 14-21; Isaiah 55:1-5; Romans 9:1-5;
Matthew 14:13-21

Materials Needed
Break pieces of bread into cups or bowls. Make sure you have one cup or bowl for every family member.

Monday

You open your hand, satisfying
the desire of every living thing. (Psalm 145:16)

Scripture Reading
Psalm 145:8-9, 14-21. After the reading, give everyone their bowl of bread pieces. You might say something like, "You may not believe this, but there are people in our world who have less to eat every day than the bread in these bowls. Imagine if this was your food for a whole day!

"God is aware of these people. The Psalmist tells us that God 'upholds all who are falling' (v. 14). We also read that 'The eyes of all look to you, and you give them their food in due season' (v. 15). If God upholds the needy and provides food for the hungry, then why are there hungry people in our world?" Allow time for response.

"God does provide, but sometimes God gives to others to share with the needy. We have more than we need. Much of the world does not have enough. God provides for the hungry by blessing us and directing us to share."

Closing Prayer
Close in a time of silent prayer. Then, thank God for providing us with all we need and more. Ask God to help us remember to share with others.

Family Journal
_____
_____
_____
_____
_____

Tuesday

Ho, everyone who thirsts, come to the waters; and you that have no money, come, buy and eat! (Isaiah 55:1)

Scripture Reading

Isaiah 55:1-5. After the reading, you might say something like, "Why would anyone keep food from hungry people, especially if there is more than enough?" Allow family members time to think about this question and offer answers.

Continue by saying, "Sometimes when people have a lot of money and things, they are afraid they will lose it. They are afraid if they don't keep a lot of extra food and other things on hand, they might go hungry. These people see all the hungry people of the world and believe there is not enough to go around. In other words, they don't believe God can provide for everybody."

Read Isaiah 55:1-5 again. Ask, "What do you think Isaiah means when he says, 'Why do you spend your money for that which is not bread?' (v. 2). These scared people with more food than they need are so empty inside that they try to fill their lives with things. And yet, they are still empty even after they buy a lot of nice things. They spend so much money on themselves, that there is none left to share bread with the hungry."

Closing Prayer

Allow everyone an opportunity to pray. Ask God to help us not be afraid. Help us to trust that if we share, there will be enough to go around.

Family Journal

_____

_____

_____

_____

_____

Wednesday

They are Israelites . . . and from them, according to the flesh, comes the Messiah, who is over all, God blessed forever. Amen. (Romans 9:4-5)

Scripture Reading

Romans 9:1-5. After the reading, you might say something like, "People who are afraid are not only stingy with bread. Sometimes they are stingy with God as well. There are people who believe that God only loves them or people like them.

"Paul was probably writing to people in Rome who thought God loved them but not the people of Israel. Paul went out of his way to assure them that God indeed loved the people of Israel because God loved all people. There is enough of God to go around too!"

Ask family members to think of groups or types of people that may be told God does not love them. Encourage creative thinking. Allow time for discussion.

Closing Prayer

Close in your worship time in prayer. Thank God for making sure there was enough of God to go around.

Family Journal

_____

_____

_____

Thursday

Jesus said to them, "They need not go away; you give them something to eat." (Matthew 14:16)

Scripture Reading

Matthew 14:13-21. (Note to parents: This story can be effectively told highlighting the themes we have identified this week. The people were hungry. The disciples did not believe they had enough to go around. Jesus told the disciples to feed the hungry. Jesus blessed what they disciples brought to him. When it was all over, every man, woman, and child was fed and each disciple had his own basket of fragments to carry away and think about.)

After the reading (or telling) of this event, ask, "What lessons can we learn for ourselves from this story? Do we have enough to share with others? Do we spend too much on things that are not bread?" Remind everyone that they each have a bowl of bread pieces, just like the disciples each had a basket. These bread pieces tell us that with God there is enough to go around.

Closing Prayer

Join hands and invite family members to pray in their own words. Ask God to help us be willing to share with others and to believe that God has already provided enough for everybody to have enough.

Family Journal

_____

_____

_____

Putting Faith into Action!

Bake some bread for friends. Deliver it warm, with a note telling them God loves them. You might also use one of the bowls that the bread pieces were in to begin collecting money to give to the cause of world hunger.

Proper 14[11]
Theme: The Lord Speaks!

Scripture Readings for the Week
Psalm 85:8-13; 1 Kings 19:9-18; Romans 10:5-15; Matthew 14:22-33

Materials Needed
Secure a small tape recorder. If you do not have one, then any sort of recorded music or song (tape, record, compact disc, etc.).

Monday

Steadfast love and faithfulness will meet; righteousness and peace will kiss each other. (Psalm 85:10)

Scripture Reading
Psalm 85:8-13. Make a recording of everyone talking. Play the tape back. Ask family members to identify each voice. (If you are using a record or tape, ask family members to identify singers by the sound of their voice.)

After fun with the recorder, read Psalm 85:8-13. After the reading, you might ask, "What does the Psalmist want to hear? (The Psalmist wants to hear the Lord speak peace.) Why would someone want to hear a word about peace?" (Because there is no peace in the world.) Continue by saying, "We can quickly identify our voices or the voices of our favorite singers, but do we recognize the voice of God. When we are tempted to hurt someone, is that the voice of God?" (NO!)

Closing Prayer
Close your worship time in a long moment of silence. Encourage family members to listen for the voice of God in our lives. After a few moments of silence, ask God for peace in our world.

Family Journal
_____
_____
_____
_____
_____

Tuesday

Now there was a great wind . . . an earthquake . . . a fire . . . and after the fire a sound of sheer silence. . . . Then there came a voice. (1 Kings 11-13)

Scripture Reading

1 Kings 19:9-18. (Note: This is a great story to tell. Emphasize how depressed and tired Elijah was. He listened for God in storms and earthquakes, but the voice of God came quietly. Elijah had to be still and quiet to hear God.) Use the recorder to illustrate how hard it is to hear a soft, quiet voice.

After the reading (or telling), you might ask, "Is it easy or hard to find a quiet place in our lives?" (Most people in our world would say it is hard to find any quiet.) Ask, "What are some of our main noise makers?" (Television, radio, electronic games, engine noises, and so on.) Continue by saying, "We may not be able to stop all the noise in our world, but we can control some of the noise in our own lives. Let's all work to find a quiet time in our daily lives so that we can listen for God's voice."

Closing Prayer

Pause for another time of silence. Make sure every noise maker possible is turned off. After a period of silence, lead in prayer asking God help us quiet things down.

Family Journal

_____
_____
_____
_____
_____

Wednesday

For, everyone who calls on the name of the Lord shall be saved. (Romans 10:13)

Scripture Reading

Romans 10:5-15. Use the recorder to make a short announcement to the family at the beginning of the worship time. You might say, "Good News! After our worship time tonight we are all going out for ice cream!"

After playing (or simply reading) the announcement, read Romans 10:5-15. You might say something like, "Ice cream is good news, but the love of God in Jesus Christ is even better news. It is the best news God has for us." Read the verses again. Emphasize verses 13-15. Continue by asking, "How does God plan for the good news to reach people? (By means of preaching.) In other words, when we tell and show the Good News, our voices and our words become God's voice for others."

Closing Prayer

Close your worship time in prayer. Thank God for using our voices to speak to others. Be sure to express thanksgiving for God's presence in our lives.

Family Journal

_____

_____

_____

_____

_____

Thursday

And early in the morning he came
walking toward them on the sea. (Matthew 14:25)

Scripture Reading

Matthew 14:22-33. After the reading, you might say something like, "The disciples of Jesus were in a pretty tough spot. Their tiny boat was no match for the wind and waves. They all knew it would not take much to overturn the boat.

"Suddenly, through the waves and wind, they saw Jesus walking on the water. They could not believe it was really Jesus and decided it must be a ghost. Between the fear created by the storm and the fear created by Jesus walking on the water, the disciples were paralyzed with fear. As we go through life, there will be times when we will be afraid. Storms or other events will come along and frighten us. We will see things we do not understand or believe, and they will frighten us. If we do not know how to deal with our fear, our fear can really hurt us or make us hurt someone else."

Ask, "How did Jesus calm the fear of his disciples?" (He spoke to them and let them know it was him.) Continue by saying, "All this week we have talked about listening for God's voice, and even serving as God's voice. Learning to hear God's words and God's voice is the way we deal with the fears of life. God says to all of us 'Take heart, it is I; do not be afraid.' "

Closing Prayer

Close your worship time in prayer. Ask God to help us learn how to listen.

Family Journal

_____

_____

_____

_____

_____

Putting Faith into Action!

Somebody your family knows would love to receive a call from you. They would be delighted to hear your voices, especially the voices of your children. They would be encouraged and affirmed by the sound of your voices. Decide who this person is and give them a call.

Proper 15[12]
Theme: People In Search of God

Scripture Readings for the Week
Psalm 67; Isaiah 56:1, 6-8; Romans 11:1-2a, 29-32; Matthew 15:21-28

Materials Needed
Using magazines, newspapers, or encyclopedias, gather pictures of people representing different ethnic and racial backgrounds.

Monday

Let the peoples praise you, O God; let all the peoples praise you. (Psalm 67:3)

Scripture Reading
Psalm 67. After the reading, show everyone the pictures you have collected. You might say something like, "These are picture of people from all around the world. They dress differently from us, they speak a different language, and in many cases, they have their own religion. They all have one thing in common with us, however God loves them and us.

"The Psalmist understood this. This psalm today is really a prayer. It is a prayer for all the people of the earth. The Psalmist wanted all these different people know God's goodness and love. If they knew this, they would praise God and give thanks."

Closing Prayer
Close your worship time. Pray that people everywhere will find God's goodness and love.

Family Journal
_____
_____
_____
_____
_____
_____

Tuesday

Maintain justice, and do what is right, for soon my salvation will come, and my deliverance be revealed. (Isaiah 56:1)

Scripture Reading
Isaiah 56:1, 6-8. After the reading, you might say something like, "The prophet Isaiah

dreamed that one day all people would find God and worship God. The prophet looked forward to a time when people from around the world would join with the people of Israel in prayer and praise."

Show the pictures to everyone again. Ask, "What makes this dream so hard to realize?" Allow time for responses. Continue by asking, "How can we make it easier for people to worship God together?" Allow time for ideas.

Closing Prayer

Close your worship time in prayer. Pray that Isaiah's dream would come true. Ask God to help us help others find their way into God's presence.

Family Journal

_____
_____
_____
_____
_____
_____
_____

Wednesday

For the gifts and the calling of God are irrevocable.
(Romans 11:29)

Scripture Reading

Romans 11:1-2a, 29-32. After the reading, you might say something like, "One of the great mistakes religious people make is believing that since God loves them, then God must hate everyone else. There was a time in the life of Paul when Christians believed that God must have rejected the people of Israel because they would not accept Jesus.

"Paul makes it clear that this idea is false, however. Simply because God's love seeks to include all the people of the world does not mean that God excludes the people God started with. All people means all people!"

Closing Prayer

Close your worship time in prayer. Ask God to help us not believe that we are loved more than anyone else. We are loved along with everyone else.

Family Journal

_____

_____

_____

_____

_____

_____

Thursday

The Jesus answered her, "Woman, great is your faith! Let it be done for you as you wish." (Matthew 15:28)

Scripture Reading

Matthew 15:21-28. After the reading, you might ask, "Why did Jesus hesitate to help this woman?" Allow for responses. You may want to point out that this woman was not a Hebrew. She was a gentile.

Continue by saying, "Jesus may have been reflecting the feelings of his disciples. What he said and did was exactly what they would have said and done. Jesus, however, did not stop with their view of gentiles. He dealt with the woman as a person of worth. Finally, he granted her request and healed her child. By this action, Jesus gave a powerful example that all people are included in the grace and love of God."

Closing Prayer

Allow everyone an opportunity to pray. Thank God for not having favorites. Thank God for loving all people the same.

Family Journal

_____

_____

_____

_____

_____

_____

Putting Faith into Action!

Take a look around your neighborhood or community. Are their people who are slightly different? What do you know about these people? Is there someone you go to school with who is from another country, or is from a different ethnic background? What could you do to let this person know that God loves them?

Proper 16[13]
Theme: How Do We Know God?

Scripture Readings for the Week
Psalm 138; Isaiah 51:1-6; Romans 12:1-8; Matthew 16:13-20

Materials Needed
Make everyone some sort of operator's license. Your own driver's license will work for you. Others may need a bicycle license or a tricycle license, very little ones may need a teething ring license. Draw pictures of yourself for the picture ID, or use real photos. Have some fun with this.

Monday

On the day that I called, you answered me,
you increased my strength of soul. (Psalm 138:3)

Scripture Reading
Psalm 138. Be sure to emphasize verses 6-8. Before the reading, make and have fun with the license making project. After the project, you might say something like, "Not only do these cards allow us to operate cars and bikes, they also serve as identification cards. We can prove who we are by showing our ID cards."

Continue by asking, "How do we know God? Does God have a license to be God? Does God have an ID card? Of course not. And yet, there are some very important identifying things about God that allow us to know God. The Psalmist was talking about God's identity in Psalm 138. The writer knew God by observing the things God did." Re-read verses 6-8. Ask, "How does the Psalmist know God?" Allow family members to respond.

Closing Prayer
Close your worship time in prayer. Ask God to help us see the identifying marks of God in our world and in our lives.

Family Journal

_____
_____
_____
_____
_____
_____
_____

Tuesday

*Look to the rock from which you were hewn,
and to the quarry from which you were dug. (Isaiah 51:1)*

Scripture Reading

Isaiah 51:1-6. After the reading, you might ask, "What did the prophet mean when he said, 'Look to the rock from which you were hewn?' Who was he talking to? What 'rock' was he talking about? The prophet was telling the people of Israel about their identity."

Continue by saying, "The people of Israel knew that Abraham was their ancestor, but God wanted to remind them that Abraham was chosen by God to be their ancestor. With Abraham, God began a new family, a new people, with a special identity. Where does all this lead? The reason we want to know God's identity is for the purpose of shaping our identity. If we are God's people, then we need to behave the way God behaves. Our identity comes from God."

Closing Prayer

Join hands and invite family members to pray in their own words. Ask God to help us shape our ID's by paying close attention to God's ID.

Family Journal

_____
_____
_____
_____
_____
_____
_____

Wednesday

Do not be conformed to this world . . . so that you may discern what is the will of God what is good and acceptable and perfect. (Romans 12:2)

Scripture Reading

Romans 12:1-8. After the reading, you might ask, "If we don't gain our identities from God, where will they come from? How will we know who we are?" Allow time for discussion. We gain identity from our families of origin, our race, gender, socio-economic level, citizenship, and religion.

After the discussion, read Romans 12:1-2 again. Ask, "How do you think we conform to the world?" We conform to the world when our identity is tied completely to the world we live in. Ask, "Why do we need to resist the identity the world gives us? If we are going to be God's people, then we must take our identity from God."

Ask, "How does Paul say we resist the conforming power of the world and transform our minds to become like God? We do so by offering our whole lives to God as living sacrifices. In other words, by living for God, and learning from God. In this way our minds are renewed and transformed our identities as well!"

Closing Prayer
Close your time of worship with a few moments of silence. Ask God to renew our minds. Ask to God to help us take our identity from God and not the world around us.

Family Journal

_____

_____

_____

_____

_____

Thursday

He said to them, But who do you say that I am?
(Matthew 16:15)

Scripture Reading
Matthew 16:13-20. After the reading, you might ask, "What was Jesus asking his followers?" Jesus was asking them if they knew his identity. What did they say? They identified him as the Messiah, the Son of God. Continue by saying,

"Jesus praised them for identifying him. By recognizing Jesus as the Messiah, the followers of Jesus were now ready to serve him and help him do his work.

"The same is true for us. Only as we recognize Jesus as Messiah can we have any part in his life. Only as we learn the identity of Jesus can we begin to change our identity and become more like him. To be the people of God, we must follow Jesus, learn from him, and share in the work he began. That is who we are. That is our ID."

Closing Prayer
Close your worship time in prayer. Ask God to help us accept our identities as followers of Jesus the Messiah.

Family Journal

_____

_____

_____

_____

_____

Putting Faith into Action!

Make new licenses for everyone. Give everyone a license to follow Jesus and learn from him. These will be your ID cards for now on.

Proper 17[14]
Theme: How Do We Say, "I Love You, God?"

Scripture Readings for the Week
Psalm 26:1-8; Jeremiah 15:15-21; Romans 12:9-21;
Matthew 16:21-28

Materials Needed
If you saved your love letters, bring a few to share during your worship time. If not, provide paper and pencils. Have everyone write a love letter to another member of the family.

Monday

For your steadfast love is before my eyes,
and I walk in faithfulness to you. (Psalm 26:3)

Scripture Reading
Psalm 26:1-8. Have fun with the love letters, or in writing love notes to each other. As everyone finishes, read Psalm 26:1-8. Continue by saying, "How can we say 'I love you,' to God? I know we can just say the words, but is that the only way? We could write God a note that says 'I love you.' Is that enough?

"The Psalmist described a very important way to say 'I love you, God.' What was it the Psalmist described?" Allow a few minutes for discussion. Continue by saying, "The Psalmist lets us know that one way to show our love for God is by doing things we know are right. If we know God expects something from us, and we do what is expected, that shows God that our love is real."

Closing Prayer
Give thanks to God for loving us. Ask God to help us show our love for God by doing things that are right.

Family Journal

_____

_____

_____

_____

_____

_____

_____

Tuesday

If you turn back, I will take you back,
and you shall stand before me. (Jeremiah 15:19)

Scripture Reading

Jeremiah 15:15-21. Begin by saying, "These are tough words from the prophet, but they are honest words." After the reading, you might ask, "What was the prophet so upset about?" Jeremiah had done all the things he was supposed to, but was suffering because of it. He was beginning to wonder if God still loved him.

Continue by asking, "Do you think there is a lesson for us here? Yes. Sometimes we suffer while we are doing the right thing, and sometimes because of the right thing. Suffering and pain may cause us to think that God does not love us. Is there anything that will make God stop loving us?" Allow family members to respond. The answer is no. God always loves us, and especially as we suffer for doing right.

Closing Prayer

Close in the time of worship in prayer. Ask God to give us courage and patience to show our love for God even in the midst of painful situations.

Family Journal

_____
_____
_____
_____
_____
_____
_____

Wednesday

Let love be genuine; hate what is evil, hold fast to what is good; love one another . . . outdo one another in showing honor. (Romans 12:9-10)

Scripture Reading

Romans 12:9-21. Before the reading, you might ask something like, "If we were going to build a community where everybody who loved God worked hard to show that love to one another, what would that community look like? How would people behave?" Allow a few moments for responses.

Read Romans 12:9-21. After the reading, you might say, "Paul offers us a picture of a community that loves God. They showed their love for God by loving each other. The world created by this love is not a perfect love. There is weeping and there is even evil (v. 21). Yet, even though the community is not perfect, it is still a community that says to God 'We love you!' "

Closing Prayer

Close in your worship time. Ask God to help make our community a place where the love of God is visible and active.

Family Journal

_____
_____
_____
_____
_____
_____
_____

Closing Prayer

Close your worship time in prayer. Thank God for loving us. Ask God to help us show our love with the living of our lives.

Family Journal

_____
_____
_____
_____
_____
_____
_____

Thursday

If any want to become my followers, let them deny themselves and take up their cross and follow me.
(Matthew 16:24)

Scripture Reading

Matthew 16:21-28. After the reading, you might say something like, "Jesus described for us the ultimate love letter. We say 'I love you, God' when we offer our lives to God. When we are willing to serve and sacrifice, when we are willing to follow Jesus, and when we are willing to be discipline and faithful, then we are showing love in a convincing behavior. We shout to the world 'I love God' by simply living the life God calls us to live."

Putting Faith into Action!

Write a love letter to God with your actions. Do something that shows your love for God. Do you know someone who is sad? Go and comfort that person. Do you know someone celebrating a victory or success? Go and celebrate with that person. Do you know someone lonely or depressed? Be a friend to that person.

Proper 18[15]
Theme: Piecing Together Good Relationships

Scripture Readings for the Week
Psalm 119:33-40; Ezekiel 33:7-11; Romans 13:8-14; Matthew 18:15-20

Materials Needed
You will need a jig-saw puzzle. (Try to get one that will take some effort to put together.)

Monday

Teach me, O LORD, the way of your statutes, and I will observe it to the end. (Psalm 119:33)

Scripture Reading
Psalm 119:33-40. Spread the puzzle pieces out on the floor or table. You might say something like, "There are sure a lot of pieces to this puzzle. How in the world will we ever get them all together to make some kind of picture."

Read Psalm 119:33-40. After the reading, you might say something like, "Life is something like a puzzle. There is a picture to life something that makes sense, something that is happy and good but life does not come to us already put together. We find life in pieces, like puzzle pieces on the table. Our main task through life is put the pieces together so that our lives look like the picture God has for us.

"As we read the scriptures this week, we will be noticing some of these pieces. What pieces of life do you hear the Psalmist talking about?" Read the verses again. Allow family members a chance to respond. The first piece of the puzzle of life for the Psalmist is to learn how God wants things done and do them that way. That is good advice. If we start off in the right direction, we will have a better chance of ending up in the right place with the right pieces.

Family Journal
_____
_____
_____
_____
_____

Tuesday

Whenever you hear a word from my mouth,
you shall give them warning from me. (Ezekiel 33:7)

Scripture Reading

Ezekiel 33:7-11. Spend a little time working on the puzzle. Try to get a few pieces of edge put together. After a few moments, read Ezekiel 33:7-11. After the reading, you might say something like, "The prophet Ezekiel offers us another important piece to our life puzzle. Can you figure out what it is?" Allow family members to respond. Read the verses again if needed.

After a brief discussion, continue by saying, "Ezekiel reminds us of the importance of telling the truth even if the truth is bad news. If I do something wrong and no one tells me because they don't want to hurt my feelings, that doesn't help me very much. If you make a mistake and I don't explain it to you, you will likely make the same mistake again.

"Now, this probably doesn't work as well on people we don't know. It is very helpful, however, if we do it with love and kindness. Telling the truth to each other is a way we show love. It is also one of the important pieces we need to build a life."

Closing Prayer

Close your worship time. Thank God for telling us the truth.

Family Journal

_____
_____
_____
_____
_____
_____

Wednesday

Instead, put on the Lord Jesus Christ, and make no
provision for the flesh, to gratify the desires.
(Romans 13:14)

Scripture Reading

Romans 13:8-14. Have some paper on a hand and a pencil. Enlist a family member to take notes later. Work on the puzzle for a while. After a few minutes, read the scripture for today. After the reading, you might say something like, "The Apostle Paul offers us quite a few pieces for our life puzzle. Let's try to list them in order."

Read the text again, slowly. Encourage family members to call out life pieces as they hear them. The first one, *love*, is obvious. The others may have to be coaxed out. Here are a few possible items for the list: *be awake, live honorably, no drunkenness, no debauchery* (needs defining for children wild partying with sexual overtones), *no quarreling*, and *no jealousy.*

The final piece Paul offers us is to put on the Lord Jesus Christ. Ask family members what they think that means. Allow time for reflection and response. Continue by saying, "Putting on Christ means to make our lives and his life one piece. To put on Christ means to become like Christ to follow and imitate him. Is that an important piece to our puzzle? Yes!"

Closing Prayer

Close in your worship time in a moment of silence. Let each family member ask God (in his or her own words) to help us put on Christ.

Family Journal

_____
_____
_____
_____
_____
_____

Thursday

For where two or three are gathered in
my name, I am there among them. (Matthew 18:20)

Scripture Reading

Matthew 18:15-20. Work with the puzzle some more. When you have finished, read the verses from Matthew. After the reading, you might say something like, "Jesus draws together several of the pieces we have already picked up. He points out the importance of being honest with each other. He also points out the importance of loving one another. Jesus, however, puts these pieces together in such a way that we are able to see a new piece to the life puzzle. Can you figure it out?" Read the verses again. Allow family members time to respond.

Continue by saying, "The new piece is found in verse 20. Jesus makes it clear that the purpose of telling the truth to each other and loving one another is to create a community, that is, a place where we can gather together. When at least two of us are gathered together, Jesus promises to be there with us. That is a very important piece to the life puzzle. Jesus does not want or expect us to go through life alone. He wants us to go with others, and he wants to go with us."

Closing Prayer

Close in your worship time in prayer. Thank God for sending Jesus into the world. Thank God for allowing Jesus to be with us as we try to put together pieces of life's puzzle.

Family Journal

_____
_____
_____
_____
_____
_____
_____

Putting Faith into Action!

Finish the puzzle. Many people live in our world with pieces of their lives missing. some have lost loved ones or friends. Others have lost their health. Still others have lost jobs, homes, or dreams. These losses can make life feel like a confused, pointless puzzle. Does your family know anyone like this? Your friendship and compassion could be an important piece to the puzzle of their lives. Offer someone you know your love and concern.

Proper 19[16]
Theme: Forgiveness

Scripture Readings for the Week
Psalm 114; Genesis 50:15-21; Romans 14:1-12; Matthew 18:21-35

Materials Needed
Cut pieces of black construction paper into odd shapes.

Monday

The mountains skipped like rams, the hills like lambs.
(Psalm 114:4)

Scripture Reading
Psalm 114. Distribute the pieces of black paper so that everyone has at least one piece. You might say something like, "These black pieces of paper stand for the things we do in our lives that are wrong. One piece might be for lies that we tell. Another black piece might be for things we say that hurt people. Still another might be for anger we have toward another person, or even violence. When we say or do things that we know are wrong, it is as though a black spot forms on the inside of us. We become trapped and feel awful."

Read the psalm. Continue by saying, "This Psalmist did not feel guilty. This was a song of someone who had felt the joy that came from being set free. The Psalmist remembered a time when the people of Israel were trapped in Egypt, but God acted to free them. There were no black spots in the Psalmist the day he wrote these words."

Continue by saying, "So how do we get rid of these black spots? That is what we will be talking about for the rest of the week. Be sure to hang on to your black spot until we figure out how to get rid of it."

Closing Prayer
Close in the time of worship in prayer. Ask God to help us find joy and beauty in life.

Family Journal

_____

_____

_____

_____

_____

_____

_____

Tuesday

Joseph wept when they spoke to him. Then his brothers also wept, fell down before him, and said, We are here as your slaves. (Genesis 50:17-18)

Scripture Reading

Genesis 50:15-21. Make sure everyone has their black spot. Spend a few moments giving them names. What are some of the wrong things we do to create these dark places in us. Allow family members enough time to name their own failure. Don't forget yours.

After a few moments, read Genesis 50:15-21. You might summarize the story by saying, "Joseph's brothers had sold him into slavery. They hated their brother and really wanted to kill him. Now, Joseph was a powerful man in Egyptian politics. Their sin (dark place) was known to everyone, especially Joseph. They were frightened. They were unsure of what Joseph would do. What did Joseph do?" Allow family members to respond. Read the verses again in necessary.

Continue by saying, "The brothers of Joseph came filled with the darkness of their dark deeds. Joseph released the darkness by simply forgiving them. That is what the word forgiveness means to release, to let it go."

Closing Prayer

Close in the worship time in a few moments of silence. Ask God to forgive us our dark places, as we forgive the dark places in others.

Family Journal

_____

_____

_____

_____

_____

_____

Wednesday

Why do you pass judgment on your brother or sister? . . . For we will all stand before the judgment seat of God. (Romans 14:10)

Scripture Reading

Romans 14:1-12. Make sure everyone has their dark spot with them. Before the reading, you might say something like, "Wouldn't it be silly if I said, 'Ha, my dark spot is not as dark as your dark spot. I am a better person than you because my spot is not as dark." Allow family members to respond.

After a few moments, read Romans 14:1-12. Continue by saying, "Paul makes it clear that we have no business thinking we are better or worse than anyone else. We are all in this together. We need to help each other, not criticize each other. We need to encourage one another, not put one another down.

"We all have dark spots in our lives, and dark is dark. God wants us to find ways to get rid of the darkness and to live in the light."

Closing Prayer

Close in prayer. Ask God to help us be kind and understanding with people who fail. Give God thanks for showing us how to live in the light.

Family Journal

_____
_____
_____
_____
_____
_____
_____

Thursday

So my heavenly Father will also do to every one of you, if you do not forgive your brother or sister from your heart. (Matthew 18:35)

Scripture Reading

Matthew 18:21-35. Carefully tell or read the parable of the unforgiving servant. Make sure you make the connection between the parable and verses 21-22. After the telling or reading, you might say something like, "When we ask God to forgive us, God immediately releases the dark spots in us and throws them away." (Throw some of the dark pieces of paper away as you speak.)

Continue by saying, "God wants us free of dark behavior and from the bad feelings that go with it. But once we are forgiven, and God has let the dark things go, then we must be willing to practice forgiveness. It is not right for God to throw my dark spot away when I won't throw your dark spots away. Because I am forgiven, I must be willing to forgive. (Take the dark spots away from everyone and throw them away.)

"God forgives us and sets us free to love one another, but we can only be free if we forgive one another."

Closing Prayer

Close your worship time in prayer. Thank God for forgiving us our sins. Ask God to help us forgive others.

Family Journal

_____
_____
_____
_____
_____
_____

Putting Faith into Action!

Spend some time in discussion about the relationships in your life. Parents, do you need to forgive children? Children, do you need to forgive your parents? Parents, do you need to forgive parents? Are there friends or co-workers who need to be forgiven? Do we need to ask forgiveness from someone? If you answer yes to any of these questions, go throw the dark spots away.

Proper 20[17]

Theme: God's Grace Getting What We Don't Deserve

Scripture Readings for the Week
Psalm 145:1-8; Exodus 16:2-15; Philippians 1:21-30; Matthew 20: 1-16

Materials Needed
Use a pay check or pay stub for the lesson study. A tax return will also work.

Monday

The LORD is gracious and merciful, slow to anger and abounding in steadfast love. (Psalm 145:8)

Scripture Reading
Psalm 145:1-8. Before reading the psalm, you might say something like, "We are going to be thinking about God's grace this week. When we talk about 'grace' we are talking about a 'gift giving nature.' " Show everyone a pay stub or display item. Say, "When we work, we earn a salary with the work we do. It is not given to us, we work for it. When someone gives us a gift, however, we have not earned it. It was given to us because of someone's gift-giving nature.

"The psalm today is about God's gift giving nature. Listen for the gifts." Read Psalm 145:1-

8. After the reading, allow family members to name the gifts they heard as the psalm was read.

Closing Prayer
Thank God for giving us so much we have not earned. Be sure to express thanksgiving for God's presence in our lives.

Family Journal
_____
_____
_____
_____
_____
_____

Tuesday

Your complaining is not against us but against the LORD. (Exodus 16:8)

Scripture Reading
Exodus 16:2-15. Before reading the verses from Exodus, you might want to set up the context. Here is a suggested summary: "God saved the people of Israel from a life of slavery and pain

in Egypt. God was leading them to a promised land.

"Along the way, the people of Israel began to have second thoughts. They began to wonder how God would be able to do all the things promised through Moses. When the people found themselves without food, they were sure they were doomed. They began to complain. They even thought that slavery was better than uncertainty, but God demonstrated God's gift-giving nature. Even in the midst of complaints, God sent food to them."

After the summary, you might ask, "How was this an example of God's grace?" (The people did not earn the food, nor do anything to make the food appear. God did it all.)

Closing Prayer
Close your worship time in prayer. Thank God for providing for our needs.

Family Journal

_____

_____

_____

_____

_____

Wednesday

For he has graciously granted you the privilege not only of believing in Christ, but of suffering for him as well.
(Philippians 1:29)

Scripture Reading
Philippians 1:21-30. Before the reading, alert family members that this scripture may be hard to believe. Encourage them to listen for the word grace or one of its forms (gracious, graciously, etc.).

After the reading, ask family members if they heard the word. Read verses 29-30 again. After identifying the word and its context, you might say something like, "This is a very strange idea. It sounds like Paul is telling us that God has given us the gift of suffering. Who would want to suffer or give a gift of suffering to another person? Imagine that we had a terrible disease. The only way we could recover from our illness was through a difficult and painful surgery. The surgery, however, is an expensive procedure. Because of this, we are unable to pay for the needed surgery. So the surgeon says, 'That's OK. I will do the surgery for free.' In that sense we would have been given the gift of the surgery. Even though it was painful, it was still a gracious gift and it saved our lives.

"The life we live in Christ is like that. Following Jesus led Paul and his friends into trouble in the ancient world. The gift Christ gave them in return, however, was eternal life and blessing. Therefore, Paul spoke of a gracious gift of suffering."

Closing Prayer
Allow everyone an opportunity to pray. Thank God for allowing us to share life with Jesus.

Family Journal
_____
_____
_____
_____
_____

Thursday

So the last will be first, and the first will be last.
(Matthew 20:16)

Scripture Reading
Matthew 20:1-16. Before the reading, you might say something like, "In order for God to deal graciously with all people, it sometimes appears that God is being unfair. Some people who live and follow Jesus for a long time suffer a great deal. Others follow Jesus only a short time, and do not suffer. And yet, both people receive the same gift. Jesus tells an important story that deals with this apparent unfairness."

After the reading, you might ask, "This is a story about work and wages. Where is the grace in the story?" (The grace is in the giving of work. Grace also appears in every person receiving the same wage even for those who did not do the same work.) Continue by asking, "How does Jesus explain the apparent unfairness of the situation?" (The field belongs to the farmer. He has the right to do with it as he sees fit. No one was cheated. If God chooses to bless those who come to grace late, that is God's business. It is also part of God's essential gift-giving nature.)

Closing Prayer
Close your time of worship in a few moments of silence. Thank God for paying us what we earn, and what we didn't earn.

Family Journal
_____
_____
_____
_____

Putting Faith into Action!

Practice the fine art of gift giving. Do one another's chores for the week end. Cook and serve a meal to one another. Make gifts or cards and share them with each other. If you can, extend you gift giving to include neighbors or friends. Cut your neighbor's yard or bake a cake and carry it to a friend.

Proper 21[18]
Theme: Learning to Obey God

Scripture Readings for the Week
Psalm 78:1-4, 12-16; Exodus 17:1-7; Philippians 2:1-13; Matthew 21:23-32

Materials Needed
Play the game Simon Says. Stress the importance of only doing what "Simon says." The game illustrates obedience.

Monday

Give ear, O my people, to my teaching; incline your ears to the words of my mouth. (Psalm 78:1)

Scripture Reading
Psalm 78:1-4, 12-16. After playing Simon Says for a few minutes, you might say something like, "God wants us to do the things God has told us in the same way we followed the rules of the game, but why should we?"

Allow family members time to respond. After a few moments of discussion, continue by saying, "Some people think we should obey God out of fear. If we don't do what God says, God will punish us. Other people say we should obey God for what God will give us for rewards. What does the Psalmist say?"

Read Psalm 78:1-4, 12-16. After the reading, continue by saying, "The Psalmist tells us that we should obey God because of what God has already done. By saving and blessing us, God has shown us that God is worthy of being obeyed."

Closing Prayer
Close your worship time in prayer. Ask God to help us learn to do the things we should.

Family Journal
_____
_____
_____
_____
_____
_____
_____

Tuesday

He called the place Massah and Meribah . . .
Is the LORD among us or not? (Exodus 17:7)

Scripture Reading
Exodus 17:1-7. After the reading, you might say something like, "The people of Israel had a hard time trusting God. They were always complaining to Moses. It takes a long time to learn that someone is trustworthy. Hearing that God was trustworthy with the people of Israel helps us a little. Until we know that God will take care of us and is truly trustworthy, however, we will have trouble obeying God."

Encourage family members to think of ways God has already shown love and blessing in your family. Parents should be prepared to begin this discussion. Assist children in seeing the care of God at their level. After the discussion, you might ask, "Is God trustworthy?" Yes. Then God is worthy to be obeyed.

Closing Prayer
Give God thanks for being so trustworthy and caring. Be sure to express thanksgiving for God's presence in our lives.

Family Journal
_____
_____
_____
_____
_____
_____

Wednesday

Let the same mind be in you that was in Christ Jesus.
(Philippians 2:5)

Scripture Reading
Philippians 2:1-13. Play Simon Says for a while. Before the reading, you might say something like, "If we decide that God is trustworthy and that we should live the way God wants us to live, how do we know how to live? In the game 'Simon Says' the leader calls out the instructions and we always know what to do. Who, then, calls out with God's instructions? We are ready to obey, but what is it we should do?"

Read Philippians 2:1-13. Encourage family members to listen carefully for the leader's instructions. After the reading ask, "Who is the leader in these verses? (Paul, read v. 12). What is the leader's instructions? (To imitate Christ.) How do we do that?" (By living as humble servants.)

Closing Prayer

Close your worship time in prayer. Thank God for giving us good leaders and teachers (and parents!). Thank God also for the example of Jesus.

Family Journal

_____
_____
_____
_____
_____
_____

Thursday

Which of the two did the will of his father?
(Matthew 21:31)

Scripture Reading

Matthew 21:23-32. Change the name of the game from Simon Says to Jesus Says. The same rules apply, however. Use some typical fun stuff (Jesus says, "Stand on one leg."). Then, mix in a few thought provoking instructions (Jesus says, "Love your neighbor.").

After a few minutes of play, read Matthew 21:23-32. After the reading, you might say, "Jesus gives us a very clear definition of obedience in this story. What is it? Who is the one who does what God wants?" (The one who obeys and acts properly is the one who obeys God.)

Closing Prayer

Close your worship time in prayerful silence. Ask God to help us obey.

Family Journal

_____
_____
_____
_____
_____
_____

Putting Faith into Action!

Learn a new game. It may be a board game or a video game. Notice the rules and objectives of the game. An alternative activity might be to attend a sporting event as a family. Discuss the rules and objectives of the game. Relate this discussion to this week's lessons.

Proper 22[19]
Theme: The Rejected Stone

Scripture Readings for the Week
Psalm 19; Isaiah 5:1-7; Philippians 3:4b-14; Matthew 21:33-46

Materials Needed
If you have Lego® building blocks or wooden blocks, these toys would be excellent. Pieces from an erector set or dominoes will also work. If all else fails, cut some paper into small squares to use as building blocks.

Monday

The heavens are telling the glory of God; and the firmament proclaims his handiwork. (Psalm 19:1)

Scripture Reading
Psalm 19. Before the reading, spend a few moments building something. Discuss how important each piece is to the whole. When you finish, you might say, "Well anyone who came to our house while we were not here would say, 'Look what they built!'"

Read Psalm 19. Continue by saying, "That is exactly what the Psalmist was doing. He looked into the heavens and looked at the cre-ated world, then and said, 'Wow, look what God made!' The Psalmist was able to move from an appreciation of the building to praise and thanksgiving for the builder."

Closing Prayer
Allow everyone an opportunity to pray. Thank God for building such a wonderful world.

Family Journal
_____
_____
_____
_____
_____
_____
_____

Tuesday

My beloved had a vineyard on a very fertile hill. (Isaiah 5:1)

Scripture Reading
Isaiah 5:1-7. Build something different from last night. Allow your children to choose the form

your building will take. After several minutes, you might ask, "What would we do if our building suddenly began talking to us? Suppose our building said, 'Hey, I don't want to be what you are making me. I want to be something else.' How would that make us feel?" Allow time for fun responses.

After a few moments, read Isaiah 5:1-7. Continue by saying, "The prophet told the people of Israel they were like a building that did not want to be what God wanted them to be. How did this make God feel?" Allow for responses. After a brief discussion, continue by saying, "By creating the universe, God has demonstrated a wonderful capacity for making things. Therefore, we can trust God to build our lives."

Closing Prayer
Close your worship time in prayer. Ask God to make our lives the kind of building best for us.

Family Journal

_____
_____
_____
_____
_____
_____
_____

Wednesday

Yet whatever gains I had, these I have come to regard as loss because of Christ. (Philippians 3:7)

Scripture Reading
Philippians 3:4-14. Start a new building. Deliberately build in such a way that your miniature structure is either not attractive or falls apart easily. After a few moments of play, read the passage from Philippians. Continue by saying, "The Apostle Paul described some of the accomplishments of his past life. He was an important man in Jewish life. He was well known and well respected. We could say that he had built for himself quite a life.

"Paul did not consider his former accomplishments important, however. They were things he had built for himself. He realized that the great things he had built for himself before he found Jesus, were actually not very sturdy after all. Only a life built around and on Jesus will hold up. Just like our building we started today, if we don't build according to God's plan, our lives will not work the way God wants them to."

Closing Prayer
Join hands and invite family members to pray in their own words. Ask God to build our lives according to the plan given to us by Jesus.

Family Journal

_____

_____

_____

_____

_____

_____

Thursday

The stone that the builders rejected has become the corner-stone, this was the LORD's doing, and it is amazing in our eyes. (Matt 21:42; Psalm 118:22-23)

Scripture Reading

Matthew 21:33-46. Continue with your building project. Try to expand your efforts. After several minutes, read Matthew 21:33-46. Continue by saying, "Jesus used the same language that the prophet Isaiah did earlier. He used the image of a vineyard to describe what was happening with God's people. God wanted to build something good and useful, but the people would have no part in it. They wanted to build what they wanted. All of us do this one way or another.

"Jesus, however, introduced an important idea to this whole building business. He stated plainly that he is the chief cornerstone. The cornerstone of any building is the most important piece. Without this stone the building will fall. Jesus said in effect, 'I am the main piece, but you have thrown me away and tried to build without me.' We cannot build the life God wants us to build without the chief cornerstone Jesus."

Closing Prayer

Close your worship time in prayer. Ask God to build something good in our lives. Ask God to help us build with the correct cornerstone.

Family Journal

_____

_____

_____

_____

_____

_____

Putting Faith into Action!

If there is new construction going on in your area, pay a visit to the site. Try to locate the key pieces of the buildings. If you know someone who is building a house or building, try to arrange a time when the builder might talk to your family about all that goes into making a building sound and strong. If none of these is possible, spend an afternoon building buildings and lives with plastic or wooden blocks.

Proper 23[20]
Theme: Many Are the Called, But . . .

Scripture Readings for the Week
Psalm 106:1-6, 19-23; Isaiah 25:1-9; Philippians 4:1-9; Matthew 22:1-14

Materials Needed
Try to locate an invitation to a wedding, graduation, or birthday party. If none of these are available, use construction paper and markers to make an invitation. Have fun with this. Invite family members to ice cream for dessert. Or invite family to clean their rooms, or work in the yard.

Monday

Remember me, O LORD. (Psalm 106:4)

Scripture Reading
Psalm 106:1-6, 19-23. If you are making invitations, have fun with that for awhile. If you are using actual invitations, show them to family members and explain how an invitation works. You might say something like, "If we are invited to attend a party or a wedding, that means that the people having the party care enough about us to want us there. They want us to share in their happiness and in their celebration."

Read Psalm 106:1-6, 19-23. Emphasize verse 5. Continue by saying, "When the Bible uses the words 'chosen ones' it means 'invited ones.' Starting with the people of Israel, God eventually invited all people to share in the blessings of God's love and mercy. An invitation from God is very similar to an invitation from anyone else. If we don't respond, we don't share in the joy." (That is what the Psalmist describes in verses 19-23.)

Closing Prayer
God invites us to be the people of God and to share a special life. For that to happen, we must respond to the invitation with obedience and faithfulness. Close your worship time in prayer. Thank God for the invitation. Use your own words to accept the invitation.

Family Journal
_____
_____
_____
_____
_____

Tuesday

Then the LORD will wipe away the tears from all faces . . . for the LORD has spoken. (Isaiah 25:8)

Scripture Reading

Isaiah 25:1-9. Review your invitations. If you did not finish making one from yesterday, take some time and finish. As you read, be sure to emphasize verses 6-9. After the reading, you might say something like, "The prophet Isaiah described the kind of party that God is inviting us to attend. It is a party where poor people have food. It is a party where people living in difficult circumstances find hope and peace. God is throwing a party where all hurting people can find healing and lonely people can find friends.

"It is hard to imagine that anyone would miss a party like this. What can we do to make sure everyone knows they are invited to come?" Allow time for responses.

Closing Prayer

Close your worship time prayers of thanksgiving. Thank God for inviting us to the party.

Family Journal

_____
_____
_____
_____
_____
_____
_____

Wednesday

Finally, beloved, whatever is true . . . honorable . . . just . . . pure . . . pleasing . . . commendable . . . think about these things. (Philippians 4:8)

Scripture Reading

Philippians 4:1-9. Review briefly the idea of invitation. After the reading, you might say, "There is always at least two ways to look at things. We can see the bad side of every thing, or we can try to see the good in everything. As you read what Paul wrote to his friends in Philippi, which of the two do you think he was encouraging?" Allow time for responses. Read the verses again if needed.

Continue by saying, "God invites us to view life and the world in a new way. God's invitation does not make bad things stop happening, but tells us that there is always another way of looking at things. Bad things don't become good things. We just learn to expect good and bad to be present at the same time we then learn to see the good!"

Closing Prayer
Close your worship time with a few moments of silence. Thank God for the invitation to see the world in a different way.

Family Journal
_____
_____
_____
_____
_____
_____
_____

Thursday

The kingdom of heaven may be compared to a king who gave a wedding banquet for his son. (Matthew 22:2)

Scripture Reading
Matthew 22:1-14. After the reading, you might want to say something like, "Verse fourteen sounds very strange to us. It almost sounds like 'Many are invited, but few actually are allowed inside.' That is not exactly what Jesus meant." Read the parable again.

Continue by saying, "The invitation to God's party goes out to everyone. Coming to God's party, however, means being willing to

change clothes to change our lives! We are invited to come, but not dressed just any old way. We are invited and encouraged to come if we are willing to respond to the invitation properly. So how does verse 14 sound now? 'Many are invited, but not many are willing to change clothes to change their lives to get in.' "

Closing Prayer
Close your worship time in prayer. Ask God to help us be willing to change our lives, to change our way of thinking so that we may come to the party!

Family Journal
_____
_____
_____
_____
_____
_____

Putting Faith into Action!

Throw a costume party for friends. Send out invitations. Be sure to include in the invitation that everyone is expected to dress up in a costume. Keep track of how many are invited and how many show up. Did anyone come without a costume?

Proper 24[21]
Theme: Give To God What Is God's

Scripture Readings for the Week
Psalm 99; Isaiah 45:1-7; 1 Thessalonians 1:1-10;
Matthew 22:15-22

Materials Needed
Collect enough coins for everyone to have one.

Monday

Extol the LORD our God . . . for the LORD our God is holy.
(Psalm 99:9)

Scripture Reading
Psalm 99. Distribute coins to everyone. Encourage family members to study them closely. Discuss the image found on the coins (Lincoln, Jefferson, Washington, etc.) Then, locate the words "In God We Trust." After a few moments, you might say, "For as long as there has been money, it has been important to people. We use money to buy food and pay our bills. Some people try to make money the 'most' important thing in life. That is a mistake. If we make money the most important thing in life we end up worshiping our money as a god."

Read Psalm 99. After the reading, you might say, "The Psalmist did not doubt who God was in his life. The writer of this psalm was not confused about who would protect and provide for the needs of people. Only God can meet our needs and provide for us. Therefore, only God is worthy of our worship."

Closing Prayer
Close your worship time in prayer or silence. Ask God to help us use money wisely and not to expect more from it than it can provide.

Family Journal
_____
_____
_____
_____
_____
_____
_____

Tuesday

I the LORD do all these things. (Isaiah 45:7)

Scripture Reading

Isaiah 45:1-7. Begin by reviewing the coins from last night. After identifying the figures on your coins, you might say, "All of the male images represented on our coins have one thing in common. Washington, Jefferson, and Lincoln all held power as presidents."

Read Isaiah 45:1-7. Continue by asking, "According to the prophet, who has the real power in the world?" Allow time for discussion. After a few moments, you might say, "There is a close connection in our world between money and power. People with lots of money are able to influence other people to get what they want. Sometimes they are even able to influence presidents. The prophet makes it clear, however, that it is really God who has the power to do things in our world. People of power are fooling themselves if they think they can do anything without God."

Closing Prayer

Close your worship time in prayer. Ask God to help us remember who has the real power in our world. Ask God to help us not be overly impressed by people who misuse wealth.

Family Journal

_____
_____
_____
_____
_____
_____

Wednesday

For the people of those regions report . . . how you turned to God from idols, to serve a living and true God. (1 Thessalonians 1:9)

Scripture Reading

1 Thessalonians 1:1-10. Emphasize verse 9. Call attention to the images on our coins. Ask, "Do you know what an 'idol' is?" (An idol is an image or statue that is used for worship purposes. Ancient people believed that their gods lived inside the idol.) Continue by saying, "In ancient times, many people believed that their rulers were gods. The images stamped on their money were intended to promote this idea. Money used to promote the worship of the king was a form of idol worship.

"The people of Israel promised God they would not worship idols. In their Covenant with God they promised to worship God only. That is why Paul is so pleased with his friends. They have turned away from idols and found the true

God." Ask, "Is it possible for us to worship idols in our day?" (Yes. If we love our money or our possessions more than God, they become idols to us.)

Closing Prayer
Allow everyone an opportunity to pray. Ask God to help us avoid idol worship. Ask God to help us worship the true and only God.

Family Journal
_____
_____
_____
_____
_____
_____
_____

Thursday

The he said to them, Give therefore to the emperor the things that are the emperor's, and to God the things that are God's. (Matthew 22:21)

Scripture Reading
Matthew 22:15-22. After the reading, you might say something like, "The Jewish people were very angry. The Roman Empire held them in slavery and forced them to pay heavy taxes. They also resented Roman soldiers in and around their worship place. Several leaders decided they would see what Jesus had to say about all this. The Roman money they were forced to use had an image of the Roman Emperor stamped on it. The Jews considered this a form of idolatry. What they really wanted, however, was to get Jesus in trouble with the Romans and get rid of him.

"The question Jesus was asked was very tricky. Either way he answered the question, Jesus would make someone mad. If he said 'pay your taxes,' the Jews would be angry. If he said 'Don't pay your taxes,' the Romans would be angry. Jesus, however, offered a common sense approach that provided for living in a world of taxes, while at the same time giving due honor to God. What was Jesus' response to the question about taxes?" Allow time for family members to respond. Read the text again if necessary. After a few moments of discussion, continue by asking, "What belongs to God?"

(Everything! Therefore, God gets our loyalty, trust, worship, and love.)

Closing Prayer
Close your worship time in prayer. Ask God to help us to worship God and not things.

Family Journal

_____
_____
_____
_____
_____
_____
_____

Putting Faith into Action!

Have a yard sale this weekend. Go through your things and decide what you need and don't need. Take any money you make and donate it to the church benevolence fund or some other relief agency.

Proper 25[22]
Theme: What It Means to Love God

Scripture Readings for the Week
Psalm 90:1-6, 13-17; Deuteronomy 34:1-12;
1 Thessalonians 2:1-8; Matthew 22:34-46

Materials Needed
Secure a piece of rope or yarn about three to four feet long.

Monday

O prosper the work of our hands! (Psalm 90:17)

Scripture Reading
Psalm 90:1-6, 13-17. After the reading, you might say something like, "The writer of this psalm was very familiar with suffering and pain. He prayed that the Lord would provide as many good days as there had been bad days. At the close of the psalm, the writer offered a simple prayer. 'O prosper the work of our hands.' For the writer of this psalm, God could best show God's love by simply blessing the work of the Psalmist and the people of Israel."

Show everyone the rope or yarn. Tie one end of it to a table or chair. Hold on to the other end with both hands. Continue by saying, "This is what the Psalmist had in mind. At one end of this rope is God. God makes everything possible. At the other end of the rope we stand. If the rope is connected to God, then our life and work will be good in God's eyes."

Closing Prayer
Bring your worship time to a close. Ask God to hold on to God's end of the rope. Also pray that God would help us hold on to our end of the rope.

Family Journal
_____
_____
_____
_____

Tuesday

. . . but you shall love your neighbor
as yourself: I am the LORD. (Leviticus 19:18)

Scripture Reading
Leviticus 19:1-2, 15-18. Begin by tying the rope or yarn to the same table or chair you used yes-

terday. You might remind family members that life and work must be tied to God if they are going to succeed. Tie the other end of the rope or yarn to another table or chair. Read Leviticus 19:1-2, 15-18.

Continue by saying, "The writer of Leviticus was well aware of our need to be tied to God, but the writer also knew that we need to be tied to each other. The verses we read today impress on us the importance of being part of a community. Being in community means being fair and treating everyone the same. A community of people that is tied to God is a community of people who love each other and take care of each other."

Closing Prayer

Close your worship time in fa few moments of silence. Ask God to help us create a community that is tied to God and to each in other in love.

Family Journal

_____
_____
_____
_____
_____
_____

Wednesday

So deeply do we care for you that we are determined to share with you not only the gospel of God but also our own selves. (1 Thessalonians 2:8)

Scripture Reading

1 Thessalonians 2:1-8. Begin by tying the yarn or string to the table or chairs. Read the verses from 1 Thessalonians. Continue by saying, "Not everyone is willing to be part of our community. There are many things in our world that keep people from loving each other or trusting each other. What are some of these things?" Allow family members time to respond. Subjects that might be mentioned include racial differences, social or geographic differences, and political or economic differences. Religion may also be a dividing force.

After a few moments of discussion, continue by saying, "Paul suggested a way to include people in community. (Read verse 8). By sharing the good news about God's love, and by sharing ourselves with other people, we show to them that they are welcome and wanted in our community."

Closing Prayer

Give God thanks for loving us. Ask God to help us find ways to include other people in our community of love and hope.

Family Journal

_____
_____
_____
_____

Thursday

On these two commandments
hang all the law and the prophets. (Matthew 22:40)

Scripture Reading
Matthew 22:34-46. Tie both ends of the rope or yarn so that the full length is stretched across the room. Remind everyone what each of the two ends represent one end is tied to God, the other is tied to a faithful community. Read Matthew 22:34-40.

Continue by saying, "Jesus was asked 'What is the greatest commandment?' This was like asking Jesus, 'What is the most important thing in the world?' Jesus gave his reply without any hesitation. What did he say was the most important thing in the world?" Allow family members to respond. Be sure to point out that Jesus took two commandments and made them one.

After a few moments of discussion, stand next to the rope or yard. Position yourself about half way between the two tied ends. Continue by saying, "Jesus helps us understand something very important about the way we are supposed to live. We are to love God on one end, and love our neighbors on the other end. That means we live our lives standing between God and our neighbors. That does not mean we are keeping God away from our neighbors. No, standing here in the middle, we try to help our neighbors find God and know the love of God." (Extend your hands so that you are touching both ties at the same time.)

Closing Prayer
Conclude by saying, "This is how we are to live. One hand touching God, the other hand embracing our neighbors in love." Close your worship time in prayer. Thank God for loving us enough to have someone reach out to us and include us in God's community.

Family Journal

_____
_____
_____
_____

Putting Faith into Action!

Make a cake, some cookies, or a big pitcher of tea or lemonade. Take them to some neighbors you do not know very well. Tell them you just wanted them to know you cared for them and wanted to do something for them.

Proper 26²³
Theme: Servant Leaders

Scripture Readings for the Week
Psalm 43; Micah 3:5-12; 1 Thessalonians 2:9-13; Matthew 23:1-12

Materials Needed
Find an apron and a serving tray. Allow different family members to serve a light snack during your worship times this week. An adult should start it off to show how it should be done. Be creative with snacks: fruit, cookies, cheese, crackers, and so on. If possible, allow the person serving to also share in preparing the snack.

Monday

Then I will go to the altar of God, to God my exceeding joy. (Psalm 43:4)

Scripture Reading
Psalm 43. Put on the apron and serve snacks before the reading. While everyone is enjoying their goodies you might say something like, God calls all of us to be servants. God expects us to show our faithfulness by serving God and by serving others. Serving God is not always easy. Our reading from the book of Psalm will make this clear.

Read Psalm 43. Emphasize verse 4. After the reading, you might say something like, "Serving God takes on many different forms. One way we serve God is through faithful worship. That is what the Psalmist meant in verse 4. The Psalmist did not want the pain and fear in his life to keep him from serving God in worship."

Closing Prayer
Close your worship time in prayer or song. Ask God to help us overcome anything that might keep us from worshiping God the way we should.

Family Journal

_____

_____

_____

_____

_____

_____

Tuesday

Therefore it shall be night to you, without vision, and darkness to you, without revelation. (Micah 3:6)

Scripture Reading

Micah 3:5-12. Have someone serve the snacks to the rest of the family. After enjoying the good food for a few minutes, read Micah 3:5-12. Continue by saying something like, "The prophet Micah had some stinging words for some of God's servants. To whom did the prophet address his harsh words?" Allow family members time to respond. Read the verses again if necessary.

Continue by saying, "Prophets, priests, judges, and rulers all of these are servants of God. Their purpose in the world is to make sure that fairness and truth exist, but in Micah's time many of these servants were greedy for money. They were willing to twist the truth or even twist fairness to anyone who would pay them a bribe.

"Serving God is a privilege. As servants of God, we are in a position to really help people. If we misuse our place of service, we can do great harm to people."

Closing Prayer

Close your worship time in prayer. Ask God to help us be servants that care more about people than we do our own selfish needs.

Family Journal

_____
_____
_____
_____
_____
_____

Wednesday

You remember our labor and toil, brothers and sisters. (1 Thessalonians 2:9)

Scripture Reading

1 Thessalonians 2:9-13. Begin by serving the goodies you have prepared. After snack time, read the scripture passage for today found in 1 Thessalonians 2:9-13. Continue by saying, "Yesterday we read the words of Micah as he criticized some of God's servants for taking advantage of people. Today we read part of a letter from Paul to one of the churches he helped start. Paul reminded his friends how hard he had worked, and how he refused to take money from them, even when they were willing to give an offering.

"Why did Paul work this way? Why did he insist on paying his own way instead of allowing the church to take care of him?" Allow family members time to respond. Read the text again if necessary. Continue by saying, "Paul wanted people to know that his interest was in helping people find the truth of God in Jesus Christ. He did not want anyone to think he was in it just to get something out of it for himself. This attitude demonstrates the heart of a true servant of God."

Closing Prayer

Close in a few moments of silence. Ask God to help us to have the heart and mind of a servant as we seek to live our lives.

Family Journal

_____
_____
_____
_____
_____
_____

people are not the ones who have a lot of wealth, power, or influence. The really great people in this world are the ones who serve others and serve God."

Read the verses again. Ask, "Does our world practice this view of greatness. Do we revere and reward people who serve?" Allow family members time to respond.

Closing Prayer

Close your worship time. Ask God to help us learn where and how we might serve others in our world.

Family Journal

_____
_____
_____
_____
_____
_____

Thursday

_The greatest among you
will be your servant. (Matthew 23:11)_

Scripture Reading

Matthew 23:1-12. After snack time, read Matthew 23:1-12. You might say something like, "Jesus carried the servant idea further than anyone. Jesus told his disciples that the really great people in the world are not the ones who stand around telling everyone what to do. Great

Putting Faith into Action!

Plan a meal for friends or relatives. Work as a family to plan the menu. During the meal, take turns serving different parts of the meal. Small children might be paired with an older sibling or a parent. Afterwards, discuss how it felt filling a servant role. Don't forget to serve God in worship this week.

Proper 27[24]
Theme: Oil For Your Lamp
A Proper View of the Second Coming

Scripture Readings for the Week
Psalm 78:1-7; Amos 5:18-24; 1 Thessalonians 4:13-18; Matthew 25:1-13

Materials Needed
If you have a working kerosene lantern, that would be a perfect teaching tool. A candle, nearly burned to the end, will also work. If you have none of these, simply use a box of matches. (Children should be cautioned never to play with matches, and only to use matches with an adult present.)

Monday

Give ear, O my people, to my teaching; incline your ears to the words of my mouth. (Psalm 78:1)

Scripture Reading
Psalm 78:1-7. Begin your worship time by lighting either a lantern, a candle, or a single match. You might say something like, "The lives we live are very much like this light. It burns bright, gives off heat, and people can see it. We must remember, however, that it does not burn forever. A life, like a light, eventually goes out.

For that reason, we must be careful to live the right way. We must also be willing to teach others how to live."

Read Psalm 78:1-7. Continue by asking, "What advice does the Psalmist have for us? How does the writer encourage us to use the light of our lives?" Allow family members time to respond. Read the verses again if needed. "The Psalmist stresses the importance of teaching the truth about God from one generation to the next from parents to children."

Closing Prayer
Close your worship time in prayer. Ask God to help parents teach their children. Help children to listen and believe the truth. Hopefully, one day our children will teach their children.

Family Journal
_____
_____
_____
_____
_____
_____
_____

Tuesday

Why do you want the day of the LORD? (Amos 5:18)

Scripture Reading

Amos 5:18-24. These are tough verses. You may want to paraphrase their meaning. Here is a suggested paraphrase. "The ancient Hebrews believed that a day judgement would come. They called this day of judgement 'The Day of the Lord.' During the time of Amos, some of the Hebrew people believed that the Day of the Lord would be a time of judgement on everybody except the people of Israel. They thought the Day of the Lord would be a great day of celebration for them a day when God would reward the people of Israel for being the people of God.

"The prophet Amos, however, saw things differently. He did not see the Day of the Lord as a day of light, but a day of darkness for everybody who had failed to live the way God wanted them to live. This was pretty shocking news to the people of Israel."

After explaining the reading, light your lantern, candle, or match. You might say something like, "Amos knew that we only have a limited amount of time to live our lives. Just like these lights will go out soon, so will our opportunities to do good things in this world. We cannot afford to waste what light we have doing things that are foolish and of no importance."

Closing Prayer

Join hand and invite family members to pray in their own words. Ask God to help use the light of our lives wisely.

Family Journal

_____

_____

_____

_____

_____

_____

_____

Wednesday

But we do not want you to be uninformed, brothers and sisters . . . so that you may not grieve as others do who have no hope. (1 Thessalonians 4:13)

Scripture Reading

1 Thessalonians 4:13-18. Light your lantern, candle, or match. Read the text for today. After the reading, you might say something like, "In this letter, Paul offered his readers some more thoughts on the Day of the Lord. In his day, some people thought that if a person died before the Day of the Lord, they would miss it. Paul, however, explained how wrong that belief was. Those who died before the end of time were already with the Lord. When the Lord

returns for the Day of the Lord, those people will come with him.

"The main point of Paul's message, however, is to keep our attention focused on what we are supposed to be doing with our lives. If we lose hope because our loved ones die, or if we think God will overlook us, or if we just get tired of working, our light may go out too soon. We cannot give up on life. Life is for living in the light."

Closing Prayer

Close your worship in silence. Ask God to help us hold onto to hope, the light of our lives.

Family Journal

_____

_____

_____

_____

_____

_____

_____

Thursday

Keep awake therefore, for you know neither the day nor the hour. (Matthew 25:13)

Scripture Reading

Matthew 25:1-13. Light your lantern, candle, or match. Before the reading, you might say something like, "Weddings were happy times for the Jewish people. They would celebrate all day and into the night. Part of the celebration included the arrival of the groom. Young ladies would stand outside the house with lanterns to light the way for the groom to enter. It was a special honor to light the way.

"The problem was knowing when the groom would arrive. The celebration did not run on a strict schedule. The groom could arrive anytime. The young ladies with the lanterns had to be careful not to let their lamps go out before the groom arrived. If they did, they would miss the celebration."

Read Matthew 25:1-13. After the reading, you might ask, "Jesus used this wedding celebration to teach us a lesson about the Day of the Lord. What is the lesson?" Allow family members time to respond. Continue by saying, No one knows when the Day of the Lord will come. If we use up our life-light playing around with things that don't matter, our lives will be wasted. We must live life wisely, using the light of our lives wisely. They won't last forever."

Closing Prayer
Close your worship time in prayer. Thank God for giving us the light of life.

Family Journal

_____
_____
_____
_____
_____
_____
_____

Putting Faith into Action!

Sit down and plan your weekend. What will you do? How will you use the light of your life? Can you find a balance of fun, relaxing things, and helpful meaningful activities? Can they be combined? For instance, if you are planning a shopping trip, is there anyone you could take with you? Is there a homebound person who would allow you to shop for her or him? Perhaps you are going to a movie. Do you know someone who needs encouragement or companionship? Maybe this person would like to go. Use the light wisely it won't last forever.

Proper 28[25]
Theme: Taking Care of God's Stuff

Scripture Readings for the Week
Psalm 123; Zephaniah 1:7, 12-18; 1 Thessalonians 5:1-11; 25:14-30

Materials Needed
You will need a handful of pennies.

Monday

To you I lift up my eyes, O you who are enthroned in the heavens! (Psalm 123:1)

Scripture Reading
Psalm 123. After the reading, show everyone the pennies. You might say something like, "I can easily hold these pennies in my hand. It causes me no strain at all. God holds our world and all the universe just as easily. The Psalmist praised God for 'sitting enthroned in the heavens.' This means that God owns and rules the universe. All that we know and see belongs to God's.

"Because God owns everything, the Psalmist asked God for mercy. God, who is powerful enough to hold worlds in the palm of God's hand, is surely powerful enough to meet our needs and take care of us. So the Psalmist called out for God to help in a time of need."

Closing Prayer
Thank God for holding us and caring for us. Ask God to help us in our times of need.

Family Journal
_____
_____
_____
_____
_____
_____
_____

Tuesday

Be silent before the LORD God! For the day of the LORD is at hand. (Zephaniah 1:7)

Scripture Reading
Zephaniah 1:7, 12-18. These are tough verses. You may want to summarize or paraphrase the reading. One interpretation might be: "Since God owns the world, then God has the right to

expect people in the world to behave a certain way. When God sees people hurting other people, or doing things to God's world that are wrong, God becomes angry. The prophet reminds all of us what we learned last week life is a light that does not burn forever. The time will come when God will ask us 'Why did you waste your life and hurt my world?' "

Hold out the pennies. Continue by saying, "These are my pennies. I can spend them, save them, or give them away. Or, I can loan them to you. If I loan them to you, I want them back at some time. I also want them back in the same condition I loaned them to you. That is how God sees us and the world. The world is loaned to us. We better take care of it. God will want it back from us one day."

Closing Prayer
Close your time of worship in prayerful silence. Ask God to help us take care of the world that is only loaned to us.

Family Journal

_____

_____

_____

_____

_____

_____

_____

Wednesday

Therefore encourage one another and build up each other, as indeed you are doing. (1 Thessalonians 5:11)

Scripture Reading
1 Thessalonians 5:1-11. After the reading, you might say something like, "The more we hear about the world coming to an end, the more frightened we may become. It is such a terrifying idea that we may be tempted to go into our houses and never come out. The message about the Day of the Lord, however, is not intended to frighten us. The message is simply a statement of the way things really are. We will not be here forever. If we are going to do anything, we must get to it now. (That was the message last week.) Also, the world is not ours. It belongs to God. We must take care of it.

"Finally, we are not here alone. We are in this world with other people. Some of these people are also frightened. We need to stand together with all people. We need to work together with all people to take care of each other and the world." Distribute a few pennies to everyone. Continue by saying, "If we each take a part, we can all work together. We need not fear the end if we will take care of things until then."

Closing Prayer

Close in your time of worship in prayer. Ask God to help us act properly towards life, death, the world, and other people.

Family Journal

_____
_____
_____
_____
_____
_____
_____

Thursday

So take the talent from him . . . (Matthew 25:28)

Scripture Reading

Matthew 25:14-30. This parable is powerful in its own right. Simply read it or tell it dramatically. Distribute a few pennies to every family member. After reading the passage, you might say, "Jesus pulls together all the important ideas we have discussed this week. Today's story illustrates how God loans us the world, and how we are expected to take care of it. After hearing this story, what do you think God wants us to do?" Allow family members time to respond.

Continue by saying, "Life is short. We cannot afford to waste it or hide it. God wants us to live our lives in such a way that the world is a better place. God loans us the world to take care of it. God also wants us to take care of each other."

Closing Prayer

Close in prayer. Ask God to help us live lives that are full and meaningful.

Family Journal

_____
_____
_____
_____
_____
_____
_____

Putting Faith into Action!

Explain to children about tithing (giving back to God a portion of our resources). Show them that one way we acknowledge that God owns the world is by faithfully giving a piece of it back each and every week. Explain how you arrive at the figure you intend to give. Allow family members to observe the whole process right down to placing the money in the offering plate. If you don't tithe, ask yourself why.

Proper 29²⁶
Theme: How Then Shall We Live?

Scripture Readings for the Week
Psalm 100; Ezekiel 34:11-16, 20-24; Ephesians 1:15-23; Matthew 25:31-46

Materials Needed
Provide paper and markers for everyone.

Monday

Make a joyful noise to the LORD, all the earth;
break forth into joyous song and sing praises.
(Psalm 100:4)

Scripture Reading
Psalm 100. Distribute paper and markers to everyone. You might say something like, "This week as we read the Bible, we are going to make a 'Life Map.' We are going to draw a map that starts where we are now in life, and also where we want to get to one day. As we read the Bible this week, we will fill in some of the places we need to go through to get where we are going.

"It doesn't matter for now where you want your life to end up. That's OK. We will all be starting at the same place, and ending at the same place. For the beginning point let's write 'Where I Am Now.' Draw a line across the page from 'Where I Am Now' and write 'Where I'm Going To Be One Day.' "

Read Psalm 100. Continue by saying, "The Psalmist provides us our first stop. What should we write on our 'Life Map?' Allow family members time to respond. Answers such as worship, praise, adoration, and so on, are what we are looking for. Continue by saying, "All right. We are on our way, and we have made a good start. The first stop on the map is worship. And that is where we are right now."

Closing Prayer
Thank God and let each family member praise God in his or her own words. Be sure to express thanksgiving for God's presence in our lives.

Family Journal

_____
_____
_____
_____
_____
_____
_____

Tuesday

I will save my flock, and they shall no longer be ravaged; and I will judge between sheep and sheep.
(Ezekiel 34:22)

Scripture Reading

Ezekiel 34:11-16, 20-24. Be sure to emphasize verses 20-22. After the reading, you might say something like, "As we travel through life, following our life map, we may become tempted to run some people off the road. We will always bump into people who are different from us, weaker than us, or slower than us. It will be easy for us to just shove these people aside and keep going. God does not want us to travel that way, however. The prophet lets us know that the weak and the slow are loved by God as much as God loves anybody else.

"So, we have found another stop on the map. We must watch for the needy, the weak, and the slow. We watch for them and do not run over them or past them. Now write 'Watch for the Needy' on your map."

Closing Prayer

Close your worship time in prayer. Ask God to help us watch out for people who may be different from us.

Family Journal

_____
_____
_____
_____
_____
_____
_____

Wednesday

God put this power to work in Christ . . .
(Ephesians 1:20)

Scripture Reading

Ephesians 1:15-23. Be sure to emphasize verses 20-23. After the reading, you might say, "Paul provides us with some more information for our map. As we make our way on the journey of life, we need to remember who is in charge. As we come to crossroads and turns, how will we decide which way to go? Today's passage tells us that 'Christ is the head.' That means Christ is in charge of our journey. We should make our decisions, our turns, only after checking with him."

Ask, "What would be some examples of how we might do this?" Allow family members time to respond. Examples might be choosing to tell the truth or lie. Other examples might be making fun of someone, or making a friend of that same person. Which would Jesus do? After a few minutes of discussion, encourage family members to write on their maps, Jesus is in charge.

Closing Prayer
Close your worship time with a prayer of praise. Thank God for sending Jesus into the world to lead and guide us.

Family Journal
_____

_____

_____

_____

_____

_____

_____

Thursday

And the king will answer them,
Truly I tell you, just as you did it to one of the least
of these who are members of my family, you did it to me.
(Matthew 25:40)

Scripture Reading
Matthew 25:31-46. Before the reading, make sure everyone has their life maps with them. After the reading, you might say, "This parable describes what Jesus will say to us on the 'Day of the Lord.' You will notice that the discussion centers around how we treated people as we lived our lives. Who are the people that Jesus was most concerned about?" Allow family members time to respond. You may want to read the parable again.

After a brief discussion, encourage everyone to look at their life maps. Continue by saying, "We have a beginning point and an ending point on our maps. We marked a stop for the weak and the slow. Now we can name the people we need to see. Mark on your map at different points along the way the different persons named by Jesus in this parable (hungry, sick, in prison)."

Allow time for this work to be done. Little ones may be drawing pictures rather than writing words. In the interest of time you may suggest that they just draw one needy person for now. They can add the others later. After they finish, read verse 40. You might say, "As we make our way through life, we will meet many people in need. If we will help these persons in need, Jesus said it will be like we were helpful to him."

Closing Prayer
Close in a few moments of silence. Then, ask God to help us see Jesus in the needy people of our world. Help us to remember that part of our life journey includes watching for these needy people.

Family Journal

_____
_____
_____
_____
_____
_____
_____

Putting Faith into Action!

Note: This week will be very close to Thanksgiving Day. There are many opportunities to work with others during this season of the year. Your church may organize food baskets. Groups in your church may volunteer time at Rescue Missions. Volunteer as a family to take part in one of these activities. If your church is not involved, then simply find a way to minister on your own. A phone call to your local Department of Human Resources will provide you with all the information you need to meet and minister to a needy family.

Thanksgiving Day

*And God is able to provide you with every blessing in abundance,
so that by always having enough of everything, you may share
abundantly in every good work. (2 Corinthians 9:8)*

The early residents of Plymouth joined Native Americans
to give thanks for the gifts of life-sustaining crops and
express gratitude to God for surviving the harsh winter.
President Abraham Lincoln introduced Thanksgiving Day
as a national holiday in 1863. Since 1941, we have celebrated Thanksgiving Day on the fourth Thursday in November.

Thanksgiving Day[27]
Theme: Thanksgiving

Scripture Readings for the Week
Psalm 65; Deuteronomy 8:7-18; 2 Corinthians 9:6-15; Luke 17:11-19

Materials Needed
The Thanksgiving meal will be today's worship tool.

Scripture Reading
Any of the texts above will provide a fitting text for reflecting on God's gifts to us. In fact, you may want to read them all. What follows is a brief worship suggestion centering around the Thanksgiving meal.

Before beginning the meal, gather family members around the table. Read the scriptures you have selected (or all of them). After the reading, you might say, "The food on this table serves as a vivid reminder of God's gracious love for us. God has made a world and filled it with good things. We are truly blessed.

"As we share this meal today, let us be thankful to God for it. Let us remember that we do not live by our own power. We live by the grace of God.

"Let us also not forget that the blessings God gives to us are not for us alone. 'To whom much is given, much is required.' We may enjoy this meal only to the extent that we are willing and ready to share our abundance with others."

Closing Prayer
Lead your family in a prayer of thanksgiving. Here is a suggested prayer:

O God of goodness and grace, we offer our thanks to you for the blessings of this table. And not this table only, but for every blessing of life that comes to us from you.

We are also grateful for family, and for the love we share with each other. Help us remember that our little family is intended to serve as a picture of what the whole world could be if we would only acknowledge you as Parent of all of us.

Help us not to forget the fallen and the needy. We eat this meal in their presence. Help us to remember that our blessings are also our responsibilities to share with others.

We thank you, O God, for life, and love, and laughter, and hope. Amen.

Family Journal

_____
_____
_____
_____
_____
_____
_____

Family Reflections for the Year

_____
_____
_____
_____
_____
_____
_____
_____
_____
_____
_____
_____
_____
_____

Notes

[1]Leading up to the Sunday between May 29 and June 4.
[2]Leading up to the Sunday between June 5 and June 11.
[3]Leading up to the Sunday between June 12 and June 18.
[4]Leading up to the Sunday between June 19 and June 25.
[5]Leading up the Sunday between June 26 and July 2.
[6]Leading up to the Sunday between July 3 and July 9.
[7]Leading up the Sunday between July 10 and July 16.
[8]Leading up to the Sunday between July 17 and July 23.
[9]Leading up to the Sunday between July 24 and July 30.
[10]Leading up to the Sunday between July 31 and August 6.
[11]Leading up to the Sunday between August 7 and August 13.
[12]Leading up to the Sunday between August 14 and August 20.
[13]Leading up to the Sunday between August 21 and August 27.
[14]Leading up to the Sunday between August 28 and September 3.
[15]Leading up to the Sunday between September 4 and September 10.
[16]Leading up to the Sunday between September 11 and September 17.
[17]Leading up to the Sunday between September 18 and September 24.
[18]Leading up to the Sunday between September 25 and October 1.
[19]Leading up to the Sunday between October 2 and October 8.
[20]Leading up to the Sunday between October 9 and October 15.
[21]Leading up to the Sunday between October 16 and October 22.
[22]Leading up to the Sunday between October 23 and October 29.
[23]Leading up to the Sunday between October 30 and November 5.
[24]Leading up to the Sunday between November 6 and November 12.
[25]Leading up to the Sunday between November 13 and November 19.
[26]Leading up to the Sunday Between November 20 and November 26.
[27]Thanksgiving Day in the United States occurs on the fourth Thursday in November. This one day worship activity is designed to add a dimension of depth to our family celebrations.